Outsiders

Outsiders

Why Difference Is the Future of Civil Rights

ZACHARY KRAMER

Oxford University Press is a department of the University of Oxford. It furthers
the University's objective of excellence in research, scholarship, and education
by publishing worldwide. Oxford is a registered trade mark of Oxford University
Press in the UK and certain other countries.

Published in the United States of America by Oxford University Press
198 Madison Avenue, New York, NY 10016, United States of America.

Library of Congress Cataloging-in-Publication Data
Names: Kramer, Zachary, author.
Title: Outsiders : why difference is the future of civil rights / Zachary Kramer.
Description: New York, NY : Oxford University Press, [2019]
Identifiers: LCCN 2018019004 (print) | LCCN 2018032206 (ebook) |
ISBN 9780190682750 (Universal PDF) | ISBN 9780190682767 (E-pub) |
ISBN 9780190682743 (hardcover : alk. paper)
Subjects: LCSH: Civil rights. | Equality.
Classification: LCC JC571 (ebook) | LCC JC571 .K655 2019 (print) | DDC 323—dc23
LC record available at https://lccn.loc.gov/2018019004

9 8 7 6 5 4 3 2 1

Printed by LSC Communications, United States of America

For Rhiannon

CONTENTS

ACKNOWLEDGMENTS

This work wouldn't have been possible without the help, in various forms, of wonderful friends, colleagues, and kind strangers: Kelli Alces, Daphne Atkinson, Cecelia Cancellaro, Brenda Cornelius, Beth DeFelice, David Gay, Debbie Gershenowitz, Betsy Grey, Zack Gubler, Craig B. Haircuth, Carissa Hessick, Andy Hessick, Jeff Kahn, Sherry Kramer, Stuart Kramer, Rhett Larson, Willy Lumpkin, Kaipo Matsumura, Marcia McCormick, Tara Mospan, Jeff Murphy, Mary Sigler, Judy Stinson, Doug Sylvester, Anders Walker, Adam Winkler, and Anonymous Reviewers (1, 2, and 3). Professors and conference participants at Florida State University, St. Louis University, Savannah Law School, Tulane Law, the University of Denver, and Wayne State University gave me wonderful feedback. Many thanks to Dave McBride, Holly Mitchell, Katie Weaver, Suganya Elango, Kate Roche, and everyone else at Oxford University Press who helped make this book a reality.

Izaak and Gittel never once complained when I chose to write instead of hang out with them. Izaak, in particular, let me write about his life. I am forever thankful for that gift. And Rhiannon is the best person I know. Hopefully we won't have to talk about this book anymore.

My colleague Mary Sigler supported this project from the start. She was an early reader, a sharp critic, and the dearest of friends. I miss her terribly. May her memory be a blessing.

My son has always had a keen sense of justice. His first test subjects were our family's many pets. Why does the one cat get to go outside but not the other? How come you greet the dog when you get home but not the cats? Why are the birds in a cage?

His ideas about equality sharpened with time, as he became aware of the injustices that occurred beyond the walls of our house. He was especially inspired by his school's lesson on Dr. Martin Luther King, Jr., part of the school's pervasive campaign to stop bullying. Deeply affected by the idea of civil rights, he wrote a song about racial equality:

> Black is black
> White is white,
> Let's all work together.
> [Chorus] 'Cuz we're all the same on the inside.

He sang the song often, each time with a different melody. Yet he never wavered from the central idea. People deserve to be treated equally because we are all, fundamentally, the same.

The song—which we have taken to calling the "Work Together" song—nicely illustrates the principle that lies at the heart of American civil rights law. Identity traits like race and sex are culturally significant but shouldn't be. At its most basic level, the goal of civil rights law is to undo deep patterns in the way people relate to one another. Although we tend to categorize people on the basis of salient identity traits—race, sex, disability, and age, among others—civil rights law spurns superficiality. It seeks to break down artificial barriers that divide people into different groups. Like the "Work Together" song, civil rights law envisions a society in which difference doesn't matter.

But difference does matter, significantly so. Each and every one of us is different in some way. The closet is no longer a metaphor reserved for gay people. Each of us has a part of our identity that, if revealed, would mark us as outsiders. Some of these closeted identities may seem trivial—not liking HBO's *The Wire*, rooting for the Chicago Cubs, preferring chain restaurants to fine dining. Other identities are more fundamental—being poor, having a disability, practicing a fringe religion. Whether immutable or fleeting, deeply held or fickle, these differences define who we are and how we relate to the world around us. Being different is universal. We are all outsiders.

The work of civil rights used to be about integrating marginalized groups into civic life, about breaking down barriers and shattering ceilings. Yet the landscape looks very different today. Inclusion is no longer the only problem. A mounting challenge facing civil rights today is accommodating difference. The new targets of discrimination are those who stand out among their peers. They face discrimination not because they belong to some disfavored group, but because they do not or cannot fit in. They are the freaks, the geeks, the weirdos, and the oddballs among us. They do strange things, say strange things, wear strange things, have strange opinions, and need strange accommodations.

Outsiders offers a new way to think about identity, equality, and discrimination. It argues for a civil rights for everyone.

Melanie Strandberg wanted to do something to show support for her sister. Both had survived cancer once before, but her sister's had returned. As a sign of solidarity, Strandberg shaved her head. "They told her chemo, and I found my clippers," she said.[1] Unfortunately, Strandberg ended up sacrificing more than her hair. She also lost her job.

Strandberg worked as a stylist in a salon located inside a casino, in a small town outside Spokane, Washington. After she shaved her head, her boss requested that she wear a wig to work. According to Strandberg, the boss gave two reasons why she needed to cover her bald head: You can't market hair products if you don't have hair, and customers might not be comfortable being around a bald woman. Strandberg responded by quitting.

In her resignation letter, which she posted on Facebook, Strandberg wrote, "I consider myself, my sister, and every bald woman out there to be strong and beautiful!"[2] She added, "I will not wear a wig to work and I will not hide my support for the so many battling this illness in the community and all over the world."[3] Supporting her sister was not just important to Strandberg; it defined her, was something that made her, her. As she explained in her letter, "I decided that I can't just support her fifty percent of the time. That's not why I did it."[4]

The perfect place to start, Melanie Strandberg's story highlights the promise and pitfalls of civil rights law. As the moral compass of American law, civil rights law has the highest of ambitions. In its quest to weed out injustice and right wrongs, civil rights law strives to make real change in how we order our society, to create harmony in an increasingly diverse and, at times, divisive community. Melanie Strandberg took a stand on behalf of her sister and cancer patients everywhere. This is the stuff that civil rights are made of.

Yet civil rights law is a blunt tool for making change. Despite its lofty aspirations, civil rights law is a remarkably narrow enterprise. Only a handful of traits get protected status, and baldness certainly isn't one of them. Melanie Strandberg's story is a stark reminder that most discrimination exists beyond the reach of the law.

What if the law could do more? What if it could reach a wider universe of discrimination? The goal of this book is to argue for a more inclusive vision of civil rights, one that focuses not on the usual subject of civil rights—stigmatized groups—but on individual experiences of discrimination. There is no denying that discrimination persists as a social problem. But it persists in a manner that is vastly different than it used to be. When Congress passed the Civil Rights Act of 1964, it could not foresee that the Melanie Strandbergs of the world would one day face discrimination. It could not predict what diversity would look like over half a century later.

Ours is an age of individuality, a time when diversity runs deeper and is more widespread than ever before. However fractured our society may seem at times, difference is the common denominator, the thing that cuts across groups and connects us as people. In his wonderful book *Far from the Tree*, Andrew Solomon explains difference as a unifying force. "Difference unites us," he writes. "The exceptional is ubiquitous; to be entirely typical is the rare and lonely state."[5] Modern discrimination is the product of a complex web of cultural norms, stereotypes, and unconscious biases. Together, these forces make discrimination messier and more individualized than ever before. Accordingly, the work of civil rights needs to be about the universal experience of being different. We need a right to personality.

Imagine a civil rights regime that seeks to carve out space for people to be themselves fully, a regime that values expressions of individuality as central to the human experience. Imagine that the law recognizes a right to shave your head; a right to be fat; a right to be open about your same-sex partner; a right to wear your hair in braids; a right to transition from one sex to another; a right to have tattoos; a right to speak a language other than English. These examples are drawn from real cases, all of which point to a common problem: Civil rights law is stuck in the past. Time and time again, discrimination claimants find themselves shut out of a legal system that still views the group as the focal point of discrimination. The future of civil rights must be about individuals, and a right to personality is the vehicle to make this happen.

If a right to personality sounds too utopian, consider that one branch of antidiscrimination law already works this way. Religious discrimination law is an outlier within civil rights jurisprudence. Unlike other areas of the law—such as race or sex discrimination—religious discrimination law strives to protect people in their capacity as individuals. There is no list of preferred religions, no set of required practices. Each person determines the substance of her own religious practice, and courts by and large defer to a person's choice. For a belief or practice to count as a religion, all a claimant needs to show is that the belief or practice is religious in her own scheme of things and that it is sincerely held. The result is a body of law that accepts a vast universe of religious practices, each as distinctive as the next. A hospital employee refused to get a flu shot because he is vegan (the flu shot is incubated in eggs). The court concluded that this was a religious belief.[6] A cashier at Costco wanted to wear face piercings in violation of the company's ban on facial jewelry. Religious.[7] A public school principal decided to homeschool his children so their classes would reflect "an aspect of God as the creator." Religious.[8] A police officer refused to take assignment guarding an abortion clinic. Religious.[9] A saleswoman at Abercrombie & Fitch wants to wear long skirts rather than short skirts and long-sleeve shirts rather than low-cut shirts that show her cleavage. Religious.[10]

Even more importantly, religious discrimination law does not define discrimination in the conventional manner. The hallmark of civil rights law is the idea that like people must be treated in a like manner. Religious discrimination law, by contrast, mandates differential treatment; it says that, if possible, a person's religion needs to be accommodated. Say an employee can't work on the Sabbath. The employer must at least try to rework the schedule to accommodate the employee's religious practice. This may not be possible. It may be too difficult to get other workers to change their schedules. Or maybe the employee requesting the accommodation is the only one who can do the job. The outcome of a given case matters less than the process that gets us there. For accommodation to work, people need to interact with one another, to discuss their needs and expectations, to find common ground.

I'm envisioning a grand conversation. Law will initiate little conversations, and little conversations beget big conversations. Real change can only come about if we engage each other, if we challenge each other to be true to ourselves and accept each other despite our differences. Civil rights law is at its most effective when it is accompanied by strong social norms favoring equality. *Brown v. Board of Education* could not, and did not, dismantle segregation all by itself. Law is a tool of change; it can only take us so far. In the end, it is up to us to work together to find common ground. To that end, this book seeks to reengineer civil rights law to facilitate difficult conversations about who we are and how we treat each other.

PART ONE

Identity

Discrimination, Old and New

The firm had made its decision.[1] Ann Hopkins would not become a partner. At least for now, as the partners had put Hopkins's partnership application on hold until next year. The fact that it wasn't an outright rejection was cold comfort. Ann Hopkins was mad, and with good reason.

Hopkins was a strong candidate. During her five years with Price Waterhouse—the professional services firm that would later become PricewaterhouseCoopers—Hopkins had been a standout in the firm's Washington, D.C., office. She was decisive and effective. She was tough. She was emerging as a leader. In support of her candidacy, the partners in D.C. released a joint statement praising Hopkins. They described her as "an outstanding professional." They hailed her "strong character, independence and integrity," and they noted that she had a "deft touch." Of particular importance was Hopkins's two-year effort to secure a $25-million contract with the Department of State. An "outstanding performance," the partners called it, which Hopkins performed "virtually at the partner level."

If the partnership decision turned on work product exclusively, Hopkins would have been an easy case. But partnership decisions are holistic. Making partner is as much about personality as it is about results, and the partners had some concerns about Hopkins's personality. She was curt with the support staff. She rubbed people the wrong way. She cursed. This wasn't some excuse ginned up to thwart her candidacy. Earlier in her career, partners advised Hopkins that she needed to improve her interpersonal skills, particularly with respect to her interactions with the support staff. She had improved, but not enough.

To gather information on candidates, the firm invited all the partners in the firm to submit written evaluations of the candidates. Hopkins's evaluations were revealing, to say the least. Partners described Hopkins as "universally disliked," "consistently annoying and irritating," and "macho." One said that she "overcompensated for being a woman." Another advised her to take "a course at charm school." One of her supporters wrote that "Hopkins matured from a tough-talking somewhat masculine hard-nosed mgr to an authoritative, formidable, but much more appealing lady ptr candidate." Some of these partners interacted with Hopkins more than others. Some of them had no direct contact with her whatsoever.

Thomas Beyer had spent a lot of time with Hopkins, perhaps the most of any partner at the firm. As her mentor, Beyer shepherded Hopkins though the partnership process. He was a trusted advisor. The two were close, friends as much as colleagues. When she learned of the firm's decision, Hopkins sought Beyer's counsel. He was candid: If she wanted to make partner in the future, she should walk, talk, and dress more femininely, wear make-up and jewelry, and style her hair. She should, in short, be more ladylike.

At the time, Price Waterhouse had 662 partners worldwide. Just seven of them were women. There were eighty-eight candidates up for partner that year. Hopkins was the only woman.

In 1991, the Department of Labor established the Federal Glass Ceiling Commission. Comprised of prominent leaders in government and the private sector, the Commission was tasked with making proposals to break down arbitrary barriers that prevent women and minorities from ascending to the upper ranks of corporate life. The culmination of the Commission's work was a 1995 report, "A Solid Investment: Making Full Use of the Nation's Human Capital."[2] The report opens by declaring that the glass ceiling "betrays America's most cherished principles." "The American dream is about opportunities for all," the report continues. "Yet the glass ceiling denies millions of Americans opportunities for economic and personal advancement." The report argues that the glass ceiling is not only discriminatory in operation, but it is bad for business. It proposes a number of recommendations, including more expansive affirmative action and diversity training programs, leading by example, and strengthening antidiscrimination laws. Whatever the method, the goal is the same: "achieving the full promise of our society by making its bounty available to all."

There are two ways of reading Ann Hopkins's story, and the first is in terms of the glass ceiling. Hopkins applied for partnership at Price Waterhouse in 1982, almost a decade before the Glass Ceiling Commission was created and thirteen years before it issued its findings. At the time, only seven women had scaled the firm's partnership structure, a mere one percent of the firm's total partnership. This alone suggests that Hopkins was not playing on a level field. But the story comes into even sharper focus when you add that Hopkins was the only female in a pool eighty-eight candidates deep. Men would make the decisions, and the decisions were mostly about men. Looking back, the problem seems obvious. The absence of women in the process is conspicuous, strongly suggesting that discrimination was afoot. But back in the early 1980s, this was not an uncommon picture. The whole idea behind the glass ceiling metaphor is that, to achieve equality, women would have to change the landscape. The glass ceiling would crack before it would shatter, and Ann Hopkins was determined to be an important first crack.

On this reading, what is Ann Hopkins's vision of equality? How was she harmed by the firm's decision? In the most immediate sense, Hopkins did not advance at work. Making partner is a big deal. It carries with it prestige and, in most cases, the prospect of transforming a person's financial circumstances. There is no question that being denied access to partnership is a tangible harm. But glass ceilings demand a more robust vision of equality. Sure, Ann Hopkins was injured by the firm's decision, but its real victims were women. The firm's decision sent the message that women were not welcome in leadership roles. In doing so, the firm fortified the glass ceiling. Ann Hopkins represented all ambitious women trying to climb the corporate ladder.

In this regard, Ann Hopkins's case is a textbook example of old discrimination. Old discrimination has two defining features. The first is that it involves issues of integration. Stories about old discrimination always go the same way: A group of people is being excluded from some benefit of public life. The remedy for exclusion is integration, and this is exactly what civil rights law seeks to do in cases of old discrimination: integrate the group, break down the barrier, and shatter the ceiling.

Note that the group is the focal point of old discrimination. The second feature of old discrimination is that it is only skin-deep. Group membership is the only thing that matters. A person becomes a victim of discrimination simply by virtue of having the disfavored trait in question.

A prominent case from the mid-1970s helps to illuminate the dynamics of old discrimination.[3] The Water and Power Department for the City of Los Angeles administered a pension fund for its employees. The Department funded the program, in part, through employee contributions. In practice this meant that the Department withheld employees' contributions directly from their paychecks. The problem was that the Department withheld more money from women's paychecks than it did from men's paychecks. The reason for this disparity was simple: Women tend to live longer than men. If they're going to live longer than men, women will need more money, so the company had its female employees pay larger sums into the system.

The discrimination revealed itself in wages. Because women had to make larger contributions to the system than men, women took home less pay than men, to the tune of almost fifteen percent. The discrimination was formal in nature, targeting women as a group. It didn't matter if a particular woman died earlier than expected. The Department didn't assess an employee's risk factors. It didn't require medical certification before withholding contributions. The only thing that mattered was the employee's sex. If you were female, you had to make the extra contributions, plain and simple.

It is easy to discount this case. After all, the case is older than I am. Part of the reason we can think of old discrimination as old is because it is rooted in our country's discriminatory past. The Civil Rights Act of 1964 was a response to longstanding practices that were baked into our culture—businesses refusing to serve black people, employers considering women only for secretarial positions, and so on. Sandra Day O'Connor couldn't find a job when she graduated from law school in 1952.[4] Despite graduating third in her class at Stanford Law School, the only law firm job she was offered was as a legal secretary. Hers is a story about segregation and exclusion, as well as courage and perseverance. At every turn, the legal profession was organized to exclude her, yet she always found a way to thrive. She was a pioneer because she had to be and because she could be. It is a privilege to work at a law school that bears her name.[5]

When I look out over my classroom, I see more female faces than male faces. There are more faces of color, more heads in religious coverings, and more bodies in wheelchairs than there were a decade ago when I started teaching. This is the trend in all of higher education, not just law schools. When I worry about my students' job prospects, it is because of market conditions, not discrimination. They have inherited a legal profession that is more inclusive than ever before. Organizations like the American Bar Association (ABA) and the Association of American Law Schools (AALS) are fully committed to making outsiders insiders. They have forceful nondiscrimination policies, policies that sweep broader than federal law. They offer regular programming about diversity and inclusiveness, targeting law students, lawyers, and law professors alike. I don't want to sound naïve about this. Some of my students will run into difficulties in their career, and some of those difficulties will stem from discrimination. But today's law students are in a better position than the lawyers who came before them, at least with respect to discrimination.

Although old discrimination is largely a thing of the past, it does still occur from time to time. And when it does, it tends to arise in large organizations. Which makes sense, as it is hard for large organizations to monitor what goes on in the far reaches of their outfit. The recent Wal-Mart litigation is a prime example.[6] Everything about the case was big. As the nation's largest retailer, Wal-Mart employs 1.4 million people across the country.[7] That makes Wal-Mart responsible for around one percent of the entire American workforce.[8] The plaintiffs in the case brought a sex discrimination claim on behalf of *all* women who have ever worked for the retail giant, something like 1.5 million women. They argued that Wal-Mart systematically discriminated against women in its pay and promotion decisions. Rather than making these decisions at the corporate level, Wal-Mart delegated them to local store managers, who enjoyed considerable discretion in these matters. The numbers painted a stark picture.[9] The plaintiffs' statistical expert found that, in hourly positions, men made $1,100 more than women each year.[10] And the wage gap was even greater in salaried management positions, where men out-earned women by $14,500.

With respect to promotions, the plaintiffs also made a strong showing of sex segregation. While women occupied sixty-seven percent of all hourly workers and seventy-eight percent of hourly department manager positions, they were significantly under-represented in salaried management positions.[11] At the assistant manager level, women held 35.7% of the jobs, and 14.3% of store managers, the next level up the management chain, were women.[12] And only 9.8% of the company's district managers were women.[13] As you go up the ladder, there are fewer and fewer female faces. This is a classic glass ceiling story.

The plaintiffs also submitted anecdotal accounts of sex discrimination. For instance, business meetings were held at strip clubs and Hooters restaurants. At meetings of Sam's Club, a subsidiary of Wal-Mart, executives frequently referred to female employees as "girls" and "little Janie Qs."[14] After complaining about her boss's favoritism toward men, a female employee was told that "God made Adam first."[15] Another learned that she should "blow the cobwebs from her make-up" and "doll up" if she wanted a better job.[16] And another was told that she belonged at home with her baby rather than at work.[17] The story that launched the litigation involved a female assistant manager who found a fellow assistant manager's W-2 lying around.[18] The document revealed that the other manager, a man, earned $10,000 more than she did. When she complained about the discrepancy, the single mother was told that the man had "a wife and kids to support."[19] After further protest, she was asked to submit a personal household budget. She did and eventually received a $40 a week raise, still significantly less than the male manager made.

Although the plaintiffs produced compelling evidence of discrimination, they never got their day in court. The Supreme Court dismissed the case on procedural grounds related to class actions.[20] Specifically, the Court held that the plaintiffs did not have enough in common to constitute a class.[21] There were too many plaintiffs, too many unique experiences of discrimination, too many possible points of departure. There was, perhaps, too much discrimination for a single lawsuit.

There is a second way of reading Ann Hopkins's situation at Price Waterhouse. Her story is as much about the perils of being an individual as it is about the glass ceiling. Ann Hopkins was an outsider not because she was a woman, but because of the kind of woman she was. She was brash, self-sufficient, and all too masculine for the partners' taste. She didn't conform to their idea of how she was supposed to look and act. She was different, it showed, and she didn't get the promotion because of it.

Like a living thing, discrimination evolves. It adapts and fills spaces. It is a product of its time. Modern discrimination is not like the discrimination of the 1960s and 1970s. Back then, discrimination targeted outsider groups. The goal of civil rights law was to achieve formal equality of the sexes, the races, and so on. Today, by contrast, discrimination is increasingly about the individual. The defining feature of new discrimination is that it targets people who do not or cannot conform to the whims of society. Difference is like a target on the back, inviting scrutiny. The pressure to be a part of something larger than yourself, to fit in, to assimilate—these are the pressure points of modern discrimination. In his masterful book *Covering*, legal scholar Kenji Yoshino discusses the shift from old to new discrimination. In our current environment, Yoshino writes, "individuals no longer needed to *be* white, male, straight, Protestant, and able-bodied; they needed only to *act* white, male, straight, Protestant, and able-bodied."[22] Note the distinction between being and doing. Modern discrimination is not so much about who you are, but about how you perform who you are. As the great sociologist Erving Goffman observed, identity is akin to a theatrical performance.[23] Like actors on a stage, we craft our identity through our interactions with others. Our language, mannerisms, and clothing, as well as the things we say and believe, work together to modify the identities we wear on our bodies.

Take Darlene Jespersen.[24] For over twenty years, Jespersen worked as a bartender in a sports bar at Harrah's Casino, in Reno, Nevada. She loved her job and did it well, earning the praise of coworkers and customers alike. Presumably, Jespersen would have worked there until she couldn't do the job anymore. Then something changed. For most of her years at Harrah's, the company encouraged—but did not require—women to wear make-up. Jespersen never did, on or off the job. Wearing make-up made her feel "very degraded and very demeaned."[25] She explained that make-up affected her self-dignity, robbing her of her "credibility as an individual and as a person."[26] Had the choice been hers, she would have always gone without make-up.

A change in policy took away that choice. In February 2000, Harrah's rolled out its "Beverage Department Image Transformation" program at twenty Harrah's locations, including Reno.[27] A key provision of the new program was the "Personal Best" initiative.[28] All employees involved in beverage service, both male and female, would wear the same uniform of white shirt, black vest, black bow tie, and black pants. All were expected to "be well groomed, appealing to the eye, be firm and body toned, and be comfortable with maintaining this look while wearing the specified uniform."[29] The men could not have long hair or wear make-up of any kind. Women, by contrast, were required to style their hair every day and wear their hair down at all times. Most importantly for Darlene Jespersen, the policy made make-up mandatory: "Make up (face powder, blush and mascara) must be worn and applied neatly in complimentary colors. Lip color must be worn at all times."[30]

Employees would be photographed looking their personal best, memorializing how they should look every day when they report for work.

Jespersen couldn't bring herself to abide by the make-up requirement. Wearing make-up, she concluded, would prevent her from being able to do her job well. In an ideal universe, she would have transferred to a different position within the company, one that wasn't subject to the make-up requirement. Unfortunately, she didn't qualify for any of the open positions that paid a salary comparable to her bartending job. Left with no other options, she quit. Imagine quitting a job you held for over twenty years—a job in which you thrived—simply because the company expects you to wear make-up. Most women would not have taken such a hard line. But Darlene Jespersen was not most women.

And that is how the courts viewed her situation. Jespersen sued Harrah's, alleging that the make-up requirement amounted to unlawful sex discrimination. Jespersen's theory of discrimination was that the make-up requirement compelled women to conform to a stereotypical standard of femininity. The case weaved through the courts, landing in the U.S. Court of Appeals for the Ninth Circuit, the federal court that hears appeals arising out of western states. The Ninth Circuit rejected Jespersen's claim.[31] It concluded that her injuries were too subjective to sustain a sex discrimination claim. She gave the court the "subjective reaction of a single employee,"[32] but what the court really wanted was evidence that the make-up requirement "would objectively inhibit a woman's ability to do the job."[33] Put another way, her complaints were too much her own. In order to state a sex discrimination claim, she needed to show that the make-up requirement was bad for all women, as a group.

There are two points to take away from Darlene Jespersen's case.[34] The first is that her allegations of discrimination fall firmly within the category of new discrimination. Although she cast her claim in terms of gender stereotypes, the thrust of Jespersen's claim was that the make-up requirement interfered with *her* ability to do *her* job. It was not that make-up was bad for women as a general matter, nor was it even that most women would find the make-up requirement problematic. The case was far more intimate than that. At its core, the central issue was whether Harrah's would let Darlene Jespersen be herself. She may have called it sex discrimination, but this was really a claim of Darlene Jespersen discrimination.

The second, more important point to take away is that civil rights law does not have the requisite language to deal with modern discrimination. Darlene Jespersen described her injury in terms of her own dignity and sense of self. What she wanted was for the court to say that her identity mattered, that the make-up requirement inhibited her ability to thrive in the workplace. The court, by contrast, made the case about sex discrimination writ large. It viewed the case through the glass ceiling, concluding that make-up was not a barrier to women's upward mobility at Harrah's. Although both Jespersen and the court were talking about sex discrimination, they were talking about it in completely different ways, almost past each other.

This is not an isolated occurrence. In fact, it has become commonplace for courts to struggle with the personalized nature of modern discrimination. The primary sticking point is the expectation—often tacit but sometimes explicit, as it was in Darlene Jespersen's case—that victims need to anchor their discrimination claims to a narrative of group subordination. They have to show, in other words, that the discrimination they face harms their group as a whole. A woman has to carry all women on her back, just as a black person has to speak for all black people. The group is the focal point of American civil rights law. To gain ground in the fight against inequality—to make change real—outsiders have to define who they are by saying they are like some group of people. But they are not like them, and that is why they are experiencing discrimination in the first place. While the universe of difference is vast indeed, civil rights law only cares about inter-group difference.

At the end of the workday on January 4, 2010, Dr. James Knight asked Melissa Nelson to join him in his office.[35] A dental assistant, Nelson had worked for Dr. Knight for over ten years. Joining them at the meeting was a pastor from Dr. Knight's church. The purpose of the meeting, Nelson soon found out, was to terminate her employment. Dr. Knight read from a prepared statement. He was firing her because he was attracted to her, and these feelings were interfering with his private life. He was afraid that he may try to have an affair with Nelson, which he did not want to happen. So he had to let her go. Nelson received an envelope with a month's severance pay.

For most of her time in Dr. Knight's office, Nelson had done well. She was good at her job and she got along with her boss. Their relationship was cordial, if friendly. Toward the end, however, things changed between them. They began texting often, concerning both work and private matters. Both had children, so a good amount of their texts were updates about their children's activities. At no time did Nelson flirt with or say suggestive things to Dr. Knight. Yet the same was not true for Dr. Knight. He frequently told her that her clothing was distracting. He said that if she saw his pants bulging, it meant that her clothing was too revealing. He said that not having sex with her would be like keeping a Lamborghini in a garage and never driving it. One time he texted her that the shirt she wore that day was too tight. Nelson responded that he wasn't being fair, and Dr. Knight replied that it was good for him that she didn't wear tight pants because then he would get it coming and going. Nelson also remembered a text from Dr. Knight where he asked how often she had an orgasm.

Dr. Knight's wife also worked in his dental office. She discovered that Dr. Knight and Nelson were texting. She confronted him and demanded that he fire Nelson. They consulted with their church's senior pastor, who agreed that Dr. Knight should fire Nelson. And so he did.

Melissa Nelson filed a discrimination claim, alleging that Dr. Knight discriminated against her on the basis of sex. Hers was not a sexual harassment claim. Instead, she argued that Dr. Knight terminated her because she was a woman. Had she been a man, she would not have lost her job.

The courts didn't see it that way. The trial court granted Dr. Knight's motion for summary judgment—a pre-trial motion that says there are no factual issues that need to be teased out at trial. The court concluded that "Nelson was fired not because of her gender but because she was a threat to the marriage of Dr. Knight."[36] And, of course, being a threat to someone's marriage is not a protected trait under existing civil rights laws.

The case then went to the Iowa Supreme Court on appeal, which agreed with the lower court's take on the case. Although Nelson did nothing inappropriate, Dr. Knight was free to terminate her if doing so would ease tension in his marriage. "The civil rights laws seek to insure employees are treated the same regardless of their sex or other protected status," the court explained.[37] And Dr. Knight's decision to fire Nelson "does not jeopardize that goal."[38] In an earlier version of its decision—which the court later withdrew—the court referred to Nelson as an "irresistible attraction."[39]

Criticism of the case was swift and unforgiving. Writing in the *New York Times,* sociologist Michael Kimmel compared the Iowa Supreme Court to a "Midwestern Taliban tribunal." Kimmel even went on to suggest that Mullah Omar—the leader of the Taliban—would approve of a male boss firing anyone who could tempt him.[40] Naomi Wolf, author of the bestselling book *The Beauty Myth*, called the decision "heinous." For Wolf, the decision confirmed *The Beauty Myth*'s core argument—that women's appearance is used against them as a diversionary tactic to prevent women from gaining ground in our society.[41] In an opinion piece for CNN's website, sociologist Pepper Schwartz called the court's decision "stupid," the product of an all-male court that is out of touch with women's working realties.[42]

This kind of outrage is understandable. Melissa Nelson got a raw deal indeed. But was it discrimination?

I asked my students this question, and their answers were surprising. A handful found the court's opinion problematic— one or two thought it deeply so—but most of them were more or less OK with the court's thinking. As they saw it, an employer should be given wide latitude to run its business as it sees fit. While they could envision real limits on an employer's decision-making, this case landed on the permissible side of the line. None of them felt this way about Ann Hopkins's case, and they were evenly split over Darlene Jespersen's case. Their responses make sense if you think of them in terms of group harms. Of the three cases, Ann Hopkins's case had the most to do with women as a group—the employer expected its female employees to be aggressive but later punished them for it. Melissa Nelson's was the most narrowly tailored of the three cases—she was the only "irresistible attraction" in the office, the only threat to her boss's marriage. And Darlene Jespersen's case falls somewhere between the two—involving an employment policy that affected all women, but one that not all women would object to.

New discrimination is messy. While old discrimination was easier to spot—and, therefore, easy to conceptualize as a legal matter—new discrimination defies easy categorization. Cases of new discrimination elicit a feeling that a wrong has been committed, but it is often hard to explain why. This is a failure of law. Civil rights law provides a legal language to describe social wrongs. The animating force behind this language is an intuition about justice, a feeling about right and wrong. Some wrongs are worse than others. Race discrimination, of course, is the principal evil our civil rights laws are designed to fight. This is why race gets the highest level of protection under the Equal Protection Clause and why employers cannot argue that race is a bona fide occupation qualification in hiring—a fancy way of saying that employers cannot refuse to consider applicants because of their race, even if race would seem to be an essential component to the job. And some wrongs are horrific but not discriminatory. In 2008, an employee brought a lawsuit alleging that his supervisor waterboarded him as a motivational exercise.[43] The idea was that the sales team should work as hard at selling as the waterboarded employee had worked at breathing. The allegations are awful but in no way discriminatory.

Civil rights law cannot right every wrong, nor should we expect it to. The question we have to reckon with is: Which wrongs matter? To answer this question, we need to decide what we want civil rights law to achieve. Does make-up matter? Should civil rights law care about beauty? What about the words we use and the clothes we wear? Or how diverse our institutions are?

Reasonable people can and will disagree about how to resolve these issues. My proposal is to focus on difference, to have civil rights law protect the aspects of our identities that set us apart from everyone else. Individuality is a weapon against conformity. All too often, outsiders face pressure to contort themselves into the mainstream. Some people simply can't conform, as they wear their difference on their bodies. Other people just don't want to conform, perhaps because doing so will be too taxing or because their identity was hard-fought and they're not willing to give it up. Imagine a civil rights regime that is a bulwark against conformity. Imagine a civil rights regime that takes as a given that all people are different in some way and that these differences define who we are and how we relate to those around us. Imagine a civil rights regime that cares about how each and every one of us, as individuals, experiences the world.

The subtitle of Ann Hopkins's autobiography is *Making Partner the Hard Way*.[44] It is a reference to the Supreme Court's landmark decision in *Price Waterhouse v. Hopkins*, which held that Hopkins was the victim of sex discrimination.[45] As for a remedy, the Court ordered the firm to reverse its decision.[46] Despite her poor interpersonal skills and her non-ladylike demeanor, Hopkins would be a partner after all.

The case was novel in its time. Up until that point, old discrimination dominated the landscape, with men and women (mostly women) using the courts to desegregate workplaces. Hopkins's case, by contrast, was more subtle than that. She charged that the firm allowed stereotypical ideas about women to seep into and ultimately dictate the partnership decision. Dr. Susan Fiske, a social psychologist from Carnegie Mellon University (now at Princeton), testified during the trial as a witness for Hopkins. She testified that the firm's method for evaluating its partnership candidates—which relied heavily on reviews submitted by partners—opened the door to stereotyping. Partners who had little, if any, contact with Hopkins could submit a review of her candidacy. One partner wrote that Hopkins was "universally disliked" by the staff.[47] A different partner wrote that Hopkins was "consistently annoying and irritating."[48] Many partners had substantial contact with Hopkins, but these partners did not. Fiske testified that such comments, while not stereotypical on their face, were likely motivated by Hopkins's uniqueness as the only woman up for partner that year.[49]

As to be expected, Price Waterhouse saw the situation differently. It argued that Hopkins's flawed interpersonal skills, and only her flawed interpersonal skills, were to blame for her failure to make partner. The firm roundly denied that stereotypes factored into the decision. Had she behaved more professionally toward support staff, it argued, Hopkins would have gotten the promotion. Presumably this is why the firm put her candidacy on hold rather than rejecting her outright. A rejection would have meant that Hopkins's career at Price Waterhouse was over. By putting her candidacy hold, however, the firm signaled that she would elevate to partner after she improved her relationships with her coworkers. In this sense, postponing her partnership was a commitment to her future at the firm.

The case wound its way through the courts, ultimately landing before the Supreme Court. In 1989, almost seven years after Hopkins lost her bid for partnership, the Court handed her a victory. In many ways, the case was easy for the Court. As Justice William Brennan wrote for a plurality of justices, "[I]f an employee's flawed 'interpersonal skills' can be corrected by a soft-hued suit or a new shade of lipstick, perhaps it is the employee's sex and not her interpersonal skills that have drawn the criticism."[50] But the Court went deeper than that, gesturing toward a broader theory of discrimination. "In the specific context of sex stereotyping," Justice Brennan wrote, "an employer who acts on the basis of a belief that a woman cannot be aggressive, or that she must not be, has acted on the basis of gender."[51] Recognizing that he was breathing new life into civil rights law, Justice Brennan added that "we are beyond the day when an employer could evaluate employees by assuming or insisting that they matched the stereotype associated with their group."[52]

Price Waterhouse v. Hopkins marks the shift from old to new discrimination. It draws a contrast between being a woman (old discrimination) and acting like a woman (new discrimination). In the eyes of the partners, Ann Hopkins fell short on the latter front. She was not the kind of woman the firm expected her to be. Recall sociologist Erving Goffman's dramaturgical theory of identity. Ann Hopkins stumbled at work because she went off script, performing her womanhood in a way that the partners found problematic. The partners wanted to cast a woman who was feminine—a woman who dressed the part, wore make-up, and walked daintily. But the woman they got didn't fit the bill. Yes, she was good at her job. But she was not good at being a woman.

This is a compelling way to think about new discrimination. In effect, the Court is carving a space for individuality. The lesson of *Price Waterhouse v. Hopkins* is that transcending norms is central to the work civil rights. Stereotypes lock people in place. They constrain authenticity. They thwart change. *Price Waterhouse v. Hopkins* provides the antidote to compelled conformity. It smooths a path for people to be themselves fully and openly. The promise of *Price Waterhouse v. Hopkins* is a legal means to make yourself visible.

In the realm of civil rights, visibility is a virtue. It is not enough that outsiders consider themselves to be different; they must articulate their identity to the world around them. Some of us wear our difference on our bodies, such as in the case of race or a physical disability. Just by existing in the world we assert who we are and how we are different. Others have an identity that rests below the surface—for instance, religious beliefs, sexuality, or political opinion. When identity is invisible to the naked eye, outsiders must take affirmative steps to make their identity known. In the case of religion, people say prayers or wear religious symbols. For sexual minorities, it might be going out in public with a partner or telling others about your sexual proclivities. A person can write their political beliefs on a bumper sticker or yard sign, or perhaps by telling others where she stands on certain issues. As I write this, sitting next to me in the coffee shop is a man wearing a matching hat, t-shirt, and tote bag that say "No on 487" (Proposition 487, which was voted down in 2014, would have replaced Phoenix's retirement plan from public pension to a private 401(k)-style plan).

Of course, the thing about subterranean identities is that people don't have to disclose who they really are. They can, in other words, be closeted. The closet metaphor—and the attendant idea of "coming out of the closet"—may have originated within the lesbian and gay community, but it has since become universal. To the extent that we can, we manage our identities—controlling information about us, emphasizing certain aspects about us, downplaying others. Sociologist Erving Goffman—the scholar who compared identity to a theatrical performance—identified three strategies people employ to manage their identity.[53] The first is conversion. This is where a person changes who they are. So, for example, a Christian becomes a Jew, or a person opposed to Proposition 487 decides he is now in favor of it. The second strategy is passing. Passing is where a person presents herself outwardly as something she is not. Gays pass as straight. Squares pass as hipsters. The sick pass as healthy. And on and on it goes. The critical feature of passing is that your audience lacks some key information about you. They think you're one thing but you're really something else.

The final strategy is covering. Of the three strategies, covering is the most commonplace yet least understood. Covering is where a person downplays her true identity. She does not deny who she is. She doesn't pretend to be something else. She just doesn't emphasize her identity. Covering is being out but not loud about it. The fellow in the coffee shop might be opposed to Proposition 487 but not decorate himself in his opinion. Anticipating a hostile crowd, a religious person may choose not to wear a piece of religious clothing, such as a turban, yarmulke, or headscarf. A working mom makes a concerted effort not to talk about her children during the workday.

These are just a few examples. The important thing about covering, however, is that it is ubiquitous. "Everyone covers," writes

Kenji Yoshino.[54] The pressure to be part of mainstream culture is something we can all relate to. Consciously or not, we bend ourselves to satisfy the wishes of others. The cost of not doing so can be severe. For Ann Hopkins, it almost cost her career.

And this is, ultimately, why the Supreme Court's decision in *Price Waterhouse v. Hopkins* is so important. If what Price Waterhouse did was discriminatory, as the Court concluded it was, then that means that identity work—the push and pull of being different—belongs in the American civil rights project.

The transition from old to new discrimination is a story about progress. Fifty years ago, when Congress passed the Civil Rights Act, there was no old discrimination or new discrimination. There was only discrimination. Fifty years from now, there very well may be an even newer form of discrimination. Justice takes time. Standing on the steps of the state capitol building in Montgomery, Alabama, at the conclusion of the Selma to Montgomery march in 1965, Reverend Martin Luther King, Jr., gave his now famous "Our God Is Marching On!" speech.[55] Answering the question raised by the title of his speech, King said, "the arc of the moral universe is long, but it bends toward justice."[56] Justice takes time because it is a moving target. Today's outsiders will become tomorrow's insiders, and new outsiders will emerge. Such is the ebb and flow of discrimination.

The transition from old to new discrimination is also a story about identity. The people we've met so far, despite their different jobs and distinct life experiences, share a common bond. They are outsiders. Some are outsiders by choice: Melanie Strandberg chose to shave her head and Darlene Jespersen refused to wear make-up. Others come by it naturally: Ann Hopkins is an aggressive person and Melissa Nelson is pretty. The root cause of their difference matters less than the way they experience their difference. For years scientists and advocates have debated the cause of homosexuality—is it a learned behavior or is it hard-wired into our DNA? This debate misses the point. Whatever the cause of homosexuality, the point is that our culture has been hostile to lesbians and gay men for a long time. Identity is a relative concept, for we define who we are in terms of how we relate to others. This is true for both the perpetrators and victims of discrimination.

As an antidiscrimination lawyer, I spend the bulk of my workday reading, writing, and thinking about discrimination. To tell the truth, it can be a thoroughly depressing way to pass the time. Every story of discrimination, harassment, and bullying is a stark reminder that people are often afraid of what they don't know. In far too many cases, difference brings out the absolute worst in people. Through my work, I have come to accept that bias is part of the human condition. We classify and distinguish. We make associations. We see difference. This is who we are, and we are hard to change. But change does happen, often in tangible ways that improve people's daily lives. Sometimes law brings about these changes. Cases like *Brown v. Board of Education*,[57] *Regents v. Bakke*,[58] and *Lawrence v. Texas*[59] were not just novel legal decisions, but learning opportunities for the whole country. Other times interaction and conversation are the primary drivers of change. Never underestimate the power of really getting to know and care about someone who has lived a life different from your own. Meaningful relationships are the lifeblood of social change.

The moral arc of the universe is indeed long, and it does indeed bend toward justice. Elsewhere in that same speech, delivered to a crowd 25,000 strong, Dr. King charged his supporters to think about the task that lay in front of them. "The road ahead is not altogether a smooth one," he said. "There are no broad highways that lead us easily and inevitably to quick solutions. But we must keep going."[60] Justice takes time, but it is worth the wait.

Ann Hopkins referred to her time away from the firm as a "sabbatical."[61] In all, her sabbatical lasted seven years—two years longer than her initial stint with the firm. While on sabbatical, Hopkins held a number of jobs, including contract work with the State Department and a full-time position at the World Bank. Her marriage fell apart. Her kids grew up. She adopted a standard poodle named George.[62]

When the case finally came to an end, Hopkins readied herself for life as a partner. Reentry was going to be difficult. A lot can happen in seven years, and both the firm and Hopkins had changed. Most importantly, though, Hopkins had to deal with her new reputation as the woman who sued her way into partnership. Navigating the politics of a new position is hard enough as it is, but to do so under such fraught circumstances—where everyone knows your name but not everyone is glad you came—is nothing short of brave. By this point, one thing was clear: Ann Hopkins was no shrinking violet.

Hopkins rejoined Price Waterhouse in the winter of 1991. She struggled to find her footing at first, but she eventually settled into place. Over the next eleven years, Hopkins had a solid career. She retired in 2002, giving up consulting to work in her garden and spend time with her family.

In 2005, Hopkins published an essay about the legacy of her case.[63] The most compelling part of the essay involves the advice she gives people who are thinking about using the courts to

remedy bad situations at work. Given her history, you would expect Hopkins to champion litigation. Yet she doesn't. If anything,
she seems almost to regret her course of action. "I got into litigation emotionally, almost on a whim. I fired the opening round
with a law suit and then I was dragged through years of appeals.
It seemed ill-advised to quit because each trial or appeal was fa-
vorable to me."[64] That was not all. Even if the person seeking the
advice didn't want to hear it, she would say, "Get on with your life,
your career, your other interests."[65]

Not what you'd expect from the hard-charging, aggressive busi-
nesswoman whose poor interpersonal skills and lack of make-up
almost spoiled her career.

Unlocking Identity

Where do bus drivers go to the bathroom? For most of us, the inner lives of bus drivers are of little concern. As passengers, our interactions with the bus driver are fleeting—a polite "hello" when we board the bus, a respectful "thank you" as we head out into the stationary world. It is easy to forget that the driver's workplace is a bus. Sure, the driver may begin and end the day at a depot, but the bulk of the driver's workday is spent on the road. So what do they do when nature calls?

For the drivers of the Utah Transit Authority (UTA), who drive the public buses in and around Salt Lake City, the answer was easy: Find a bathroom along your route.[1] Mindful of the natural constraints on its drivers, UTA expected its drivers to use public restrooms or, if one wasn't available, to use a restroom at a business. After all, a driver can't simply diverge from the bus's predetermined route, as there is a schedule to keep. And a driver can't waste time trying to find a public bathroom. People depend on public transportation; they need it to do what it's supposed to do, when it's supposed to do it. Surely UTA's policy makes sense, a workable solution to a practical problem. Yet the policy didn't work for everyone. One driver in particular couldn't abide by the policy, and not for lack of trying. The problem was that UTA couldn't figure out who she was.

Krystal Etsitty began working for UTA in 2001.[2] UTA operates a fixed route bus system, meaning that the busses service specified stops or stations. As a new driver, Etsitty did not have a regular route. Instead, she started as an extra-board operator, basically a substitute driver who fills in for other drivers who are out sick or on vacation. In that role, she drove most of UTA's 130 routes. It was good experience for a new driver, enabling her to learn on the job, as well as assimilate into the work culture at UTA. After she completed her ten-week probationary period, without incident, UTA hired her in an official capacity. Like her fellow drivers, Etsitty used restroom facilities along her route.

So it must have come as a major shock when she was called into her supervisor's office to answer questions about her genitals, and then to lose her job because of her answers.

Krystal Etsitty is transgender. She identifies as a woman. Like many transgender people, she has always believed that she was born with the wrong anatomical sex organs. Although born male with the given name "Michael," Etsitty had been living outwardly as Krystal for many years before she was diagnosed with Gender Identity Disorder. At the time she went to work for UTA, she was under the care of an endocrinologist, who prescribed female hormones, a standard step in the process as one prepares for sex reassignment surgery.

For most of us, finding and using a bathroom is not a significant life experience, something we mostly take for granted. For a transgender person, however, the bathroom is everything.

Civil rights law is in the business of identity. No area of law
cares more about who a person is than civil rights law. Indeed,
the entire enterprise rests on the idea that certain identities deserve special protection against discrimination. Set aside for the
time being that only *certain* identities receive this protection, as
we will return to this point in the next chapter. For now, focus
on this: Identity is a legal concept. It is something the law can
determine.

Take, for instance, the racial determination cases of the nine-
teenth and early twentieth centuries.[3] In a formally segregated
environment, where rules explicitly draw racial boundaries, there
must be some mechanism to decide a person's race. So the courts
do the heavy lifting, generating rules to determine a person's race.
Consider some examples. In 1866, the Michigan Supreme Court
held that a man with less than a quarter black or African blood
was white.[4] The case involved a challenge to Michigan's constitution, which limited the right to vote to "white male citizens."[5]
The defendant, a mixed-raced man, had been charged with illegal
voting. It was determined that, with only one-sixteenth black
heritage, he was white and should have been allowed to vote.[6]

A North Carolina court, in 1857, ruled that a "negro" was
someone with at least one-sixteenth black or African blood.[7]
The case involved a law that prohibited free blacks from carrying
guns. At the time, freedom was not the same as citizenship. As
black people were not citizens, the states could greatly restrict
their rights, including the right to own and carry weapons. The
defendant, a mixed-race man, was found with a shotgun, in violation of the gun law. In the end, the man was determined to be
black.[8]

Arkansas, meanwhile, adopted the notorious "one-drop" rule to determine race. In a 1922 case, a court said that *any* trace of black or African blood would make a person black.[9] The case involved public schooling. Arkansas schools were segregated along racial lines. The law in question gave the school district full discretion to determine if a child was white or black, and to send the child to the appropriate school. The suit was brought by a father on behalf of his children, who had been assigned to go to an all-black school. The man claimed that his kids were, in fact, white and should have gone to the all-white school. The man lost his bid to reverse the school district's decision.[10]

Race was not always decided by blood quantum. Sometimes it was more a matter of how a person looks. The infamous *Rhinelander v. Rhinelander* case of 1925 is instructive.[11] The case concerned Kip Rhinelander's suit to annul the marriage to his wife, Alice. Kip, a white man, was the son of a New York high society family. Alice, meanwhile, was the daughter of working-class immigrants. Even more importantly, she was biracial, born to a white mother and a black father. At first, the two hid their relationship from Kip's family, knowing they would disapprove of such a relationship. In time, however, Kip's family learned of the union and, as expected, disapproved of it. A mere month after the couple married, Kip—presumably at his family's urging—sought an annulment. The basis for the annulment was deception. Kip claimed that Alice hid her race from him, that she was passing as white. This was his path out of the marriage. Say she wasn't who he knew her to be.

Here's where the case gets interesting. Had Alice challenged Kip's allegations about her race—in other words, had she convinced the court that she was, in fact, white—the two could have stayed together. Kip's family may not have approved of Alice's working class roots, but at least they would have been a same-race couple. And although many states prohibited interracial marriage, New York did not. The barrier to their union was not legal; it was social, the double helix of racial and socioeconomic oppression.

So Alice should have argued that she was white, and the two would have stayed together, which is what Alice wanted anyway. But her lawyer didn't make that argument. He argued that Alice was black, that Kip went into the relationship with his eyes wide open, that he knew who Alice was and what it meant to marry her.

The critical moment of the trial came when the judge, the attorneys, and the jury retired to the judge's chambers to view the most important piece of evidence—Alice's body. At her lawyer's insistence, Alice took off her clothes, revealing her arms, legs, chest, and shoulders to the group of white men gathered in the room. They needed to see her skin as Kip saw it so many times before. Their intimacy would be their undoing. It would be clear to all in the room that Alice did not look white. Ignore the fact that Kip knew Alice's family, that he had spent considerable time with them, even lived with them for a short period. No, her body told the truth. She looked black.

Identity is a legal concept. By legitimizing their marriage, the court determined Alice's race for her, without regard to how she saw herself. As a technical matter, Alice prevailed. If Kip wanted to end the marriage, the two would have to divorce. Implicit in this holding is a statement about Alice's race. She was black. The court said so.

When Krystal Etsitty applied to work at UTA, she listed her name on the application as "Krystal Etsitty," though some of her supporting documents, such as her Social Security card, reflected her birth name, "Michael."[12] During her interview, Etsitty was asked whether she preferred to be called Krystal, the name on her application, or Michael, the name on her Social Security card.[13] She responded that most of her friends call her Mike, which was fine by her.[14] Dressed in khakis and a shirt, Etsitty wore a little bit of makeup to the interview and had medium-length hair.[15] Presumably, no one at UTA put together that Etsitty is transgender. There were signs that her identity was in flux, however. Once on the job, the badge on Etsitty's uniform read "Krystal," but she was known around the workplace as "Mike."[16]

About a year into the job, Etsitty reached out to her immediate supervisor to discuss her situation. She explained that she is transgender, that she was in the process of transitioning, and that she wanted to present herself at work as a woman. The supervisor offered support, paving the way for Etsitty to be herself fully during her shifts. To that end, she wore women's clothes, as well as makeup, jewelry, and acrylic nails. And, like any other female driver, she used women's restrooms along her route.

Word spread throughout the department that a male driver was wearing women's clothes. The rumor reached the operations manager, Etsitty's supervisor's supervisor. As she saw it, a man using the women's room was a liability issue. This could alienate their customer base. It could spoil UTA's reputation in the community. After all, Etsitty would be wearing a UTA uniform. What would people think?

Together with a human resources manager, the operations manager sat down with Etsitty to discuss the bathroom issue. The meeting was a fact-finding mission, in search of two pieces of immensely private information. First, they wanted to know where she was in the sex change process. Second, they wanted to know if she still had a penis.[17]

This is an experience that is common for transgender people and uncommon for almost everyone else. Most people go their whole lives without talking about their genitals with their boss. Most people enjoy a comfortable umbrella of privacy that shields them from such conversations. Transgender people don't have that luxury; they are without an umbrella to protect them from the elements. In our culture, transgender is synonymous with genitalia. Indeed, the one thing everyone knows about transgender identity is that it revolves around a person's relationship to his or her sex organs. Outsiders bear the burden of being different. For transgender people in particular, fielding questions about genitals is the cost of doing business.

At the meeting, Etsitty answered their questions honestly. Sex reassignment surgery is very expensive, often prohibitively so, as it usually costs upwards of $20,000. Etsitty planned to have the surgery when she could afford to. For the time being, though, she still had a penis.

They had heard enough. Following the meeting, the managers placed Etsitty on administrative leave. Later, they fired her. The stated reason for their decision was the potential for liability. The risk was too great; the company was not willing to accommodate her bathroom needs.[18]

UTA never received a single complaint about Etsitty's appearance or bathroom use. Nor did it receive any complaints about her driving.

Let's stick with the bus driver theme a little while longer. Bruce Anderson was a bus driver in Orange County, California.[19] His employer, the Orange County Transportation Authority

(OCTA), entered into an arrangement with fast food chain Carl's Jr., whereby OCTA drivers would give riders coupons for free hamburgers. The purpose of the promotion was to increase ridership, especially among young people. A burger for the price of bus fare—not a bad deal.

Anderson had a problem with the promotion. He was a vegetarian with a beef.[20] As Anderson saw it, he was paid to drive a bus, not kill cows. "I told them that I don't eat dead cows and no one else needs to either," he said. "I told them that I wouldn't support Carl's Jr. in their slaughtering of cows."[21] Half an hour later, as he reached a stop along his route, OCTA officials met his bus with a replacement driver ready to take the wheel. Ordered off the bus, in front of his passengers, Anderson was suspended indefinitely without pay. From OCTA's perspective, the promotion was part of Anderson's job. Refusing to participate was an act of insubordination.

Anderson hired famed civil rights lawyer Gloria Allred, who filed a lawsuit on his behalf.[22] Allred also filed a complaint with the Equal Employment Opportunity Committee (EEOC), a federal agency that enforces workplace discrimination laws. The EEOC issued a decision in the case, finding that OCTA's actions were discriminatory. In light of the EEOC's findings, OCTA decided to abandon its defense of the lawsuit. The parties reached a settlement out of court, under which OCTA agreed to pay Anderson $50,000. "This sends a message to other employers that they can't discriminate," Allred said of the settlement. "Employees don't leave their civil rights at the door."[23]

So the critical question: If this was discrimination, what kind of discrimination was it?

Religious discrimination. The key here is that civil rights law adopts a view of religion that is at once broad and flexible. It is broad because it reaches the whole universe of religious faith. Christians and Satanists, devout believers and atheists—all are on equal footing with respect to protection against religious discrimination. And it is flexible because it adapts to a person's faith. Take the case of the Taco Bell employee who was fired for refusing to cut his hair. The employee was a practicing Nazarite, a religion based on references in the Torah to people who abstain from a number of life activities. One of those life activities is cutting your hair. The employee's supervisors asked him to cut his hair to comply with the restaurant's grooming policy. He refused, citing his religious faith. A lawsuit followed. The defendant—a company that owned several Taco Bell franchises—settled with the employee for $27,000.[24]

Or consider the moving company in Virginia who refused to hire an applicant because he wore his hair in dreadlocks. He sued, claiming that, as a devout Rastafarian, cutting his hair would dishonor Jah, the higher power in his faith. The parties reached a settlement, awarding the Rastafarian $30,000.[25] And then there is the Internal Revenue Service (IRS) agent in Texas who was denied entry to work because she wore a kirpan. One of the five articles of Sikh faith, a kirpan resembles a small sword. A kirpan is not a weapon; it has a rounded or blunt edge. After being denied entry, the IRS declared the employee absent and stopped paying her. It later fired her. She sued, alleging religious discrimination. The matter settled after the agent earned some early victories in the litigation.[26]

Vegetarianism, long hair, dreadlocks, and a small sword. Why does civil rights law treat religion in this way?

The answer lies in the First Amendment to the United States Constitution. The First Amendment guarantees two rights relating to religion. The first is the right to exercise one's religion freely. Negative in nature, this right provides a check on government power. It prevents the government from interfering with a person's religious practice. This is why a school can't compel a Jehovah's Witness, or anyone else for that matter, to say the Pledge of Allegiance.[27] And it is why a city can't pass a law that permits Kosher butchering but forbids ritual slaughter in Santeria.[28] Of course, as no right is absolute, the right to free exercise has its limitations. Perhaps the most important limitation is the distinction between the freedom to believe and the freedom to act.[29] The freedom to believe is absolute; it is a longstanding principle of American law that our beliefs are ours to hold, and the government has no place in our heads. The freedom to act, by contrast, is at times severely restricted. A person may believe that God demands human sacrifice. Believing that is fine; acting it out is not.

The second right relating to religion comes from the First Amendment's Establishment Clause. This right amounts to a promise that the government will not pass laws that favor one religion over the other. The establishment protection is crucial in a pluralistic society like ours. The basic idea is that all religious faiths are welcome, and no system of belief should be given priority over any other.[30] Like a lot of constitutional provisions, the Establishment Clause is nice in theory but hard to patrol in practice. Think of religious displays in public spaces, prayer in school, and public funding for religious-based social services. These are hard issues that frequently divide communities. For our purposes, however, the critical point about the establishment of religion is its underlying goal: to accommodate the vast universe of religious faiths in our country.

Back to Bruce Anderson, the vegetarian bus driver. Why was refusing to distribute hamburger coupons a religious issue? To answer this question, all you have to do is combine the government's goal to accommodate religious pluralism and its wish not to interfere with religious practice. The law's overwhelming stance on religion is one of liberal neutrality—liberal in its acceptance of difference, neutral in its attempt to accommodate. The law goes out of its way not to define religion, as a person's faith is not for the government to decide. Rather than try to define what is and is not religious, the law focuses instead on the sincerity of belief. If a person sincerely holds the belief, it is religious, plain and simple. But that doesn't resolve the issue of which beliefs should count as religious.

Here the law says that, to be religious, a belief or practice need not be religious in the conventional sense. What matters is that the belief or practice is religious in the person's own scheme of things. In other words, the question is not whether other people view a belief or practice as religious; the question is whether the person making the claim considers the belief or practice to be religious. This is why strongly held moral and ethical beliefs, such as the belief that animals should not be killed for human use, can be considered religious for purposes of civil rights law. Bruce Anderson, our vegetarian bus driver, thought it wrong for humans to kill and eat animals. He clung to this belief as one would cling to a religious belief—deeply, sincerely, and without regard for how others viewed it. When his supervisors tried to get him to participate in the promotion, they were not asking him to hand out little slips of paper. They were asking him to sacrifice his faith.

And this is why his story matters. It reveals an important lesson about identity, namely, that identity is something we must determine for ourselves. We decide what we want, who we want to be with, why we do the things we do. Ultimately, we decide who we are. I have become very fond of the way Andrew Solomon refers not just to identity, as if identity is a stand-alone concept, but to the "search for identity."[31] It captures the volitional dimension of identity. Though we are all born a certain way, wearing traits given to us by our parents, we still make choices about who we want to be and how we want to experience the world. We can see this in the case of Alice Rhinelander, who passed as white both before and after she met Kip Rhinelander. Born into a mixed-race family, Alice chose to present herself as white; it was her way to avoid social stigma. And we can likewise see it in Krystal Etsitty's case. She made countless decisions about how she wanted to experience the world, not the least of which was her decision to transition from one sex to another, as well as her decision about how she wanted to assimilate into life at UTA, first as Mike and later as Krystal. In both of their cases—Alice's and Krystal's—the law isn't the only force determining identity. They are also determining their identity for themselves.

Is it true you self-identify as straight?

The student had barged into my office, interrupting a meeting between me and my research assistant. The student was worked up, practically out of breath, with an intense look in his eye. He caught me in a lie. He figured out my truth. He was there to make things right. Or so he thought.

I answered yes and invited him to sit down. I was a little rattled, to be honest, and my research assistant was annoyed by the spectacle. But we were in it now, committed to seeing this through to the end. The student collapsed in a chair, as if the confrontation took his last bit of energy. His manner began to change. He became sad, like he was mourning the death of a gay role model. Death by heterosexuality.

At the time, I was teaching as a fellow—a kind of baby law professor—at UCLA School of Law. I was hired by the Williams Institute, an academic think tank that studies sexual orientation and the law. Part of the Williams Institute's mission involves training young legal scholars who study law and sexuality. They join the faculty for a few years so they can get a head start teaching and writing before they land a tenure-track position. My class that semester was a course called Law & Sexuality. Both the student and my research assistant were in the course.

I asked the student why he thought I was gay. His answer will always stay with me. "Because of your clothes," he said. I didn't see it coming. Nor did my research assistant, who grumbled his annoyance with what was happening. "My clothes?" I asked in the most sympathetic voice I could muster, trying not to make the student feel worse. You could tell he was beginning to feel foolish. He mumbled something about my shoes, trailing off without finishing the thought.

Good teachers are always on the lookout for teachable moments, and I wanted to be a good teacher. So I engaged. I got him to see that the class was the source of his confusion. A class about law and sexuality is, in large part, a class about gay people.

Sure, we talked about other issues of sexuality, but the bulk of the class was about same-sex marriage and parenting, gays in the military, and criminal sodomy laws. The textbook I assigned is called *Sexual Orientation and the Law*. Students don't assume that their Business Organizations professor is a corporation. But they do assume that their Feminist Jurisprudence professor is a feminist and their Jewish Law professor is a Jew. It's not unreasonable to assume that the guy teaching a class on gay people is himself a gay person. My shoes, whatever it was about them, merely confirmed the conclusions he had already drawn about my sexuality.

I could go on and on about moments in my career when I have had to come out as straight. A colleague once sat me down to give me advice about how to deal with my homosexuality in the classroom. A different colleague once encouraged me not to hit on men who were applying to be professors at the school. And another colleague phoned to congratulate me on my wedding and remind me that my same-sex marriage was not a legal marriage. In the world of injustices, these are small-time problems. Truth be told, I relish the opportunity to tell these stories. Academics love stories about other academics behaving badly. More than that, though, I like to tell these stories because they all ended in the same way—with a conversation. Some of these conversations were harder and more awkward than others. But most were productive.

Too often, we leave matters of identity to speculation. We let our assumptions guide us. We lose sight of others, even as we're looking directly at them. Although it was a strange experience for me, my interrupting student did us both a service. He didn't let his doubts nag at him. We heard each other out. We talked about why appearances can be deceiving, and why appearances matter.

We talked about the role of allies in civil rights campaigns. And, yes, we talked about shoes. He left my office energized, bolting out the door as fast as he had barged through it.

After she was fired from UTA, Krystal Etsitty turned to the courts for help. She filed a sex discrimination claim against UTA. The gist of her claim will seem familiar. Etsitty argued that, like Ann Hopkins before her, she was the victim of unlawful sex stereotyping. More specifically, Etsitty argued that she was fired because she failed to live up to UTA's expectations about how a man is supposed to look and act. UTA expected a man to dress like a man, look like a man, and, most importantly, use the men's restroom. Etsitty was not that kind of man.

Not that kind of *man*? Did you notice the sleight-of-hand? Etsitty fought incredibly hard for her *female* identity. She did the medical, psychological, emotional, social, and financial work of transforming herself. She put the time in to make herself whole. Why would she tell the court she was a man? And worse, why did she make the case about being a man in a women's restroom? All that identity work seemingly down the drain.

Transgender claimants occupy an awkward position in civil rights jurisprudence—at once inside and outside the law. In most jurisdictions throughout the country, gender identity is not a protected trait. This means that, in most cases, transgender claimants cannot bring a claim for transgender discrimination. Nor can they bring a claim for disability discrimination. Although the Diagnostic and Statistical Manual of Mental Disorders-recognizes Gender Dysphoria as a diagnosable medical disorder,[32] the Americans with Disabilities Act (ADA) and the Rehabilitation Act—the leading disability discrimination statutes—explicitly exclude transsexualism and gender-related disorders from their coverage.[33] This was the result of a political compromise needed to get these laws passed.

So many transgender claimants turn instead to a sex discrimination theory. They argue that gender identity discrimination is not distinct from sex discrimination, but an example of sex discrimination. To discriminate on the basis of gender identity, they argue, is to make a classification on the basis of sex. If an employer cannot fire an employee because she is a woman, then an employer cannot fire an employee because she used to be a woman or because she has become a woman. Transgender claimants reject the idea that sex is limited to the man/woman binary. Some view sex as a continuum, with people plotted on different points between man and woman. Others view sex as a constellation, with a limitless array of configurations.

Watch how this argument plays out in a real case from the 1980s, one of the first discrimination cases involving a transgender claimant.[34] Kenneth Ulane was a commercial airline pilot with many years of experience, both in the military and with his employer, the now-defunct Eastern Airlines. Ulane took a leave of absence from Eastern, during which he underwent sex reassignment surgery. When Ulane returned to work, he returned as Karen Ulane, a female. Eastern promptly dismissed her. Ulane sued the airline, arguing that this was a classic case of disparate treatment. The only way to explain the airline's actions was sex discrimination. The airline was willing to employ a man but not a woman, and the man and woman are the same person.

Krystal Etsitty made a similar argument, but the court didn't buy it.[35] Neither did the court in Karen Ulane's case. [36] Few courts have been willing to go down this road. The problem is a framing issue. What the claimant sees as sex discrimination, the defendant sees as transgender discrimination. And while the former is actionable, the latter is not. Most courts view this through the lens of history, focusing on how "sex" got into the Civil Rights Act.[37] Representative Howard Smith, a conservative Democrat from Georgia, chaired the powerful House Rules Committee. Smith was opposed to the proposed to the Civil Rights Act, so much so that he hatched a plan to derail the entire thing. Rather than lead a frontal assault on the bill, however, Smith waged a covert campaign. He proposed an amendment to the bill that called for adding "sex" as a protected trait. Up to that point, the proposed Civil Rights Act was aimed primarily at combating race discrimination. Smith's amendment, he believed, would stop the bill in its tracks. The prospect of sex equality would prove to be too much, too soon, and the Civil Rights Act as a whole would fall.

Of course, Smith's strategy didn't go as planned. The Civil Rights Act became the law of the land, with "sex" standing proudly alongside the other protected traits. Yet many courts have latched onto this story as a means to limit the reach of the Civil Rights Act. Specifically, these courts focus on timing. Smith's amendment came at the last possible moment, as the bill was being debated on the floor. There were no reports on sex discrimination, no formal findings about what the effect of adding "sex" would be. Legislatively speaking, "sex" was a blank slate. Statutes are meant to be read. Legislatures write the law, and it is up to courts to interpret them. In doing so, courts tend to be cautious. Every now and then a court will flex its muscles and issue a decision that initiates a drastic shift in the law. But most of the time courts approach legal change gradually, with an eye toward consistency. Such is the nature of our common law tradition, which explains why most courts are not willing to say that the prohibition on "sex" discrimination covers transgender people. They presume that, when it gathered in 1963, the 88th Congress would not have meant for the Civil Rights Act to cover transgender discrimination.

There are two problems with this story. First, it's not historically accurate. In an article in the *Harvard Law Review*, legal historian Cary Franklin digs deep into the legislative history of the sex amendment.[38] Although debate over the amendment only lasted for an afternoon, the record shows that Congress had a very good idea about what was at stake. Indeed, the record reveals a sophisticated discussion about gender politics, women's protective legislation, and the role of the family in public policy. Clearly, Congress knew what it was getting itself into.

A second problem with the story is how it misconstrues the idea of legislative intent. Smith's reasons for promoting the amendment may have been suspect, but that doesn't tell us much about why Congress adopted the amendment. Smith was a powerful legislator, to be sure, but he was only one of 535 legislators in Congress at the time. The idea of congressional intent is shaky to begin with. The idea that a body of that many individuals can speak with a common voice, motivated by a singular intent, has never made much sense to me. Legislating is more art than science. A more likely story is that proponents of sex equality used Smith's bias against him. They saw an opening and went for it. His ploy failed but theirs worked. And it's a good thing it did. The passage of the Civil Rights Act is a signal moment in our country's civil rights history, a profound statement about American values, a pivotal step down the path toward equality.

None of this is to say that courts must regard gender identity discrimination as a form of sex discrimination. Some judges may not be willing to go down this route. Others may find it liberating. It's just that the sex discrimination argument isn't getting a fair shake, and that means that transgender claimants are being denied a possible path to justice.

Which brings us back to the stereotyping theory from *Price Waterhouse v. Hopkins*. Based on sheer numbers, the stereotyping theory is the strongest argument for transgender claimants, as it is the only argument that provides a viable route to recovery. But it comes at a significant cost. To take advantage of this theory, transgender claimants must align themselves with their birth sex, effectively canceling out the identity they wear in real life. For Krystal Etsitty, this meant arguing, in effect, that she was a man all along. Once in court, she ceased to be a woman. She ceased to be transgender. She was a man who wore women's clothing.

To be clear, I don't blame Krystal Etsitty for making this argument. She felt wronged and she wanted relief. The stereotyping theory was her best shot, so she molded herself to fit the law. We've already seen cases where the law determines identity. The transgender cases are an example of where the law mangles identity.

The opening scene in Jess Row's novel *Your Face in Mine* tells of a chance encounter between two old friends from high school, Kelly and Martin.[39] The two men haven't seen each other in some time, and Kelly strains to recognize Martin. He seems vaguely familiar, yet Kelly can't place him in his past. They weren't particularly close in high school, though they did spend time together. They played in a band. Kelly dropped Martin off at home once. Why couldn't Kelly remember him?

Picking up on his friend's confusion, Martin lays it out for him: The Martin from high school is gone. His last name changed from Lipkin to Wilkinson. And his race changed from white to black. Martin underwent racial reassignment surgery. Together with dialect lessons and a new backstory, the surgery corrected Martin's "racial identity dysphoria syndrome," a self-diagnosed condition.[40] A black man born in a white man's body, Martin had finally found his true self.

Your Face in Mine is a novel about what it means to become someone else. It is also about how people respond to change. As he struggles to understand what Martin has done, Kelly wonders, "There are so many parts of myself that I can change, that I have changed, but who spends much time assessing the givens?"[41] *Your Face in Mine* imagines a world where race is no longer a given. In his new skin, Martin downplays the work it took to make him his newly authentic self. "A lot of nipping and tucking," he says. "You'd be surprised at how little it takes to make a difference."[42]

Your Face in Mine is a work of fiction, but it sheds light on a central problem in American civil rights law: change. A foundational logic of equality law is that some identities are capable of change and others just are what they are. But we should be wary of this sort of distinction. What if the givens are not absolute? What if they're subject to change?

Later on in the novel, Martin opens up about his transformation. "Look at me, Kelly. I'm *black*," he says. "Black and never going back. Listen to me, I sound like some kind of crazy missionary."[43]

"No, not a missionary" Kelly responds. "A convert."[44]

Conversions are a natural part of life. People change all the time. Liberals become conservative, hardcore fans abandon their favorite pastimes, city dwellers move to the country, vice versa, and so on and so forth. Of course, some identities are harder to change than others. Before we were married, my wife converted to Judaism. She took classes, attended synagogue regularly, and became close with our rabbi. This was not a change she took lightly. The amount of time, effort, and thought she put into her conversion reflected its significance in her life. And some identities should be hard to change but aren't. I was a vegetarian for a little over a decade. Vegetarianism was an important part of my life, something I cared about deeply. Then one day I didn't. No grand revelation about food for me. It just seemed like the right time to make a change. This is further proof that identity is what we make of it.

I'm very interested in how the law responds to shifting identities—when it accepts a shift, when it doesn't, and how to reconcile those situations. So far we've focused mostly on transgender cases. Let's get at the issue from another angle. Take the basic facts of Krystal Etsitty's case but change one key element. Say that instead of transitioning from male to female, she was converting from Christianity to Islam. Say that when she went to speak to her supervisor, it was to get permission to be open about her new religious faith. Maybe she wants to wear a hijab, take breaks to pray during the day, and attend Friday prayer service at a local mosque. And say that she is fired because of this.

Would this be religious discrimination?

Of course it would. In fact, it would be an easy case. When it comes to matters of faith, we accept movement. People convert, they question, they stray from their faith, they return to the flock. Religion is outfitted for change.

Disability is another trait that has a certain amount of malleability built in. While some disabilities are lasting, others are transitory. And medical technology has created the means to change the way people experience certain impairments. Cochlear implants in the deaf community are a perfect example. For some, cochlear implants are a means to cure deafness—in other words, to convert a deaf person to the hearing world. Others see implants as a threat to deaf culture, something akin to forced conversion therapy for a gay person. The ADA recognizes that some disabilities come and go. That's why it protects people from discrimination both if they are currently impaired and if they have a history of impairment, even thought they might not be impaired at the time.[45] Determined to sweep as broadly as possible, the ADA even protects unimpaired people who are regarded as having a disability, making it possible to have a claim for mistaken disability discrimination.[46]

Something is going on here. The law anticipates change in matters of faith. And it is prepared for impairments to change over time. Why does it stumble over sex changes? Imagine what it would do with Martin Wilkinson's racial conversion.

Civil rights law is science fiction. The central issue in every discrimination case is whether the wrongdoer had discriminatory intent. The technical name for this is causation, in the sense that there is a nexus between what the wrongdoer did and what the wrongdoer was thinking. The problem is that causation is an elusive concept. The law has no real mechanism to identify discriminatory intent. Though it may have been commonplace during the era of Jim Crow, today wrongdoers rarely announce their bias. Unless the wrongdoer explicitly says something like, "I didn't hire you because of your race," the law has to ferret out discriminatory intent. Put another way, the law has to read people's minds. This is science fiction—bad science fiction.

Take a simple example. Say that an employee is late for a shift. The employer has a strict attendance policy: If the employee is late one more time, the employee will lose her job. She arrives late the following day and is fired. The employee believes that she is the victim of sex discrimination. Had she been a man, she thinks, she wouldn't have lost her job. How does she prove causation?

The easiest situation would be if her supervisor said, "I'm firing you because you are a woman." Easy, right? He told her why he was firing her. Causation requirement satisfied, no need to peer into anyone's mind.

Let's make it a little harder. Rather than candidly admitting to discrimination, say the supervisor said something suspect as he was letting her go. "I knew this was going to happen. Women are always late." This sort of statement isn't dispositive by itself, but it strongly suggests that discrimination is afoot. The employee will argue that the statement is a good reflection of what the supervisor was thinking when he fired her. And the supervisor will say that the statement is beside the point; she was fired because she was tardy, plain and simple. Then it is up to the factfinder—be it judge or jury—to settle the point for them.

Now for the hardest yet most realistic situation. Say the supervisor fired her and left it at that. How will the employee prove causation? This is where things get complicated. Without some indication of a suspect motive, the employee will have to piece together causation from the circumstances. Maybe the supervisor didn't fire a male employee who was repeatedly late. Or maybe he has a bumper sticker on his car that says "There's a Feminist in My Trunk." At best, these are circumstantial evidence of discrimination, not direct proof. The reason the law accepts this sort of evidence is because it can't get what it's really looking for. Because it can't read minds.

Whichever route the employee goes down, one thing remains consistent throughout: Civil rights law evaluates discrimination

from the perspective of the wrongdoer. Indeed, the whole enterprise is designed to figure out what the wrongdoer was thinking
when he fired the employee. The Supreme Court has invented a
slew of legal rules that try to get at this question—to peer into
the mind of the wrongdoer.[47] In application, these rules manifest
as an elaborate burden-shifting process, in which the claimant
offers evidence of discrimination, the defendant responds with
a nondiscriminatory explanation for its decision, and then the
claimant argues that the defendant's explanation is pretextual.[48]
Like an evidentiary tennis match, the litigants volley back and
forth, hoping the other side will make an unenforced error.
A court may decide that discrimination occurred—that the
wrongdoer had the discriminatory intent—or it may be convinced that the wrongdoer was not, in fact, a wrongdoer at all.
None of this is scientific. The law is not really equipped to make
these sorts of determinations.

UTA viewed Krystal Etsitty as a man who used the women's restroom. And that became her identity. That she saw herself as female was not relevant to the legal inquiry. The case was about
how UTA saw her, not about how she saw herself. Identity is
property, and this is identity theft.

What if civil rights didn't work this way? Imagine that, instead
of determining identity, civil rights law deferred to a person's
sense of self. As things stand now, religion is the one area where
civil rights law doesn't interrogate religion. It gives everyone,
believers and nonbelievers alike, the space to develop an identity of their own choosing. Authenticity comes from the inside.
Each person's search for identity—to borrow Andrew Solomon's
phrase[49]—is hers alone. Religious discrimination law gives people
space to find their faith for themselves, on their own terms. Some

do this by being part of a larger group. Others do it by defining themselves in opposition to a group. And some go their own way. The unifying thread is sincerity. Sincerity is what matters. Sincerity is what's missing from the rest of civil rights law. Krystal Etsitty was sincere in her desire to live life as a woman, just as Bruce Anderson was sincere in his opposition to eating animals. Even Martin Wilkinson, fictional though he may be, was sincere about his racial transformation. The stories in this book are as much about sincerity as they are about difference. Civil rights law decides which differences matter and when. Sincerity is the right way to think about that inquiry.

We can unlock identity. Religious discrimination law shows us the way.

The unfortunate thing about Krystal Etsitty's story is that she did everything right. She was honest about her circumstances and tried to make things work within UTA's structure. When she decided it was time to reveal the truth about her identity, she made an appointment with her supervisor, in the hope of getting his support. This was an act of bravery. It takes guts to admit to being different. Every time I wear short sleeves to a work-related function, I think about the tattoos on my arms. What will people think? Should I cover them up? When people tell me they are considering getting a tattoo in a visible spot, I encourage them to think about the situations when they will want to hide the tattoo. It is only natural to be ambivalent about difference.

But Krystal Etsitty cared enough to come clean. This is exactly how we want outsiders to handle these sorts of situations—to engage and explain, to find common ground. Litigation was her fallback, a last resort. And litigation only ever gives a partial victory. Even the winner loses something. One theme I try to drill into my students, especially my first-year students, is that litigation should be a last resort. Law should be a safety net, something we turn to when we can't work things out on our own.

People have an incredible capacity to change, to become more accepting of difference, to reconsider the way they see the world. But change doesn't happen on its own. There needs to be a spark. Conversations about identity can provide that spark.

Boxes

Dawn Dawson was an outsider among outsiders.[1] A self-described masculine lesbian woman, Dawson worked as a hair assistant and stylist trainee at Bumble & Bumble, a high-end salon in New York City.[2] The staff was an eclectic mix of outsiders, and salon management encouraged employees to wear their difference openly. The result was a workplace unlike most others, a veritable rainbow of human experiences. There were people of different races, different sexual orientations, different gender identities, people who had piercings, people with tattoos. On most days, Dawson wore leather pants and a jean jacket.[3] She wore her hair in a mohawk cut.[4] She referred to herself as a "dyke."[5] The general manager of the salon, Dawson's supervisor, was a transgender woman who began her tenure at Bumble & Bumble in the 1980s as a "shampoo boy."[6] This was not your father's workplace.

Though surrounded by difference, Dawson stood out among the crowed. She couldn't fit in with her coworkers. They teased her and called her names. They said she acted too much like a man and that she needed to act more like a woman. They called her "Donald" within earshot of clients. One of her coworkers told her that she needed to get fucked by a man. Another said that she wore her sexuality like a costume, whatever that means. And another called her "dyke."[7]

Less than two years after joining the salon, Dawson was fired and kicked out of the salon's stylist training program. The salon manager delivered the news. According to Dawson, the manager said that Dawson "seemed unhappy,"[8] and that Dawson's appearance was a problem. Specifically, as to Dawson's appearance, the manager said that the salon would not be able to place Dawson in a stylist position outside New York City. "People won't understand you. You'll frighten them."[9]

After she lost her job, Dawn Dawson sought to make things right. She sued the salon, alleging both sexual orientation and sex discrimination. These were two distinct claims, grounded in different laws. The sexual orientation claim arose under the New York Human Rights Law, a state law that treats sexual orientation as a protected trait.[10] The sex discrimination claim was based on Title VII of the Civil Rights Act, a federal statute. Regarding the latter claim, Dawson followed Ann Hopkins's lead. Like Hopkins before her, Dawson argued that she faced discrimination because she didn't look and act the part of a feminine woman.

As you would expect, Bumble & Bumble saw the case differently. The salon argued that the real reason Dawson was let go was because of a bad attitude and poor work performance. Regarding her attitude, the salon noted that customers and coworkers alike complained about Dawson's demeanor, calling her rude, abrupt, disrespectful, and hostile. Employers may be willing to look the other way when an employee is difficult personally, provided the employee is really good at her job. Bumble & Bumble did not think much of Dawn's work performance, however, which made her attitude all the more problematic.

Most lawsuits never make it to trial. Either the parties reach a settlement before trial or the judge dismisses the case before a jury can get its hands on it. Dawn Dawson's case was dismissed at the summary judgment phase of litigation. If the purpose of a trial is to find facts, to determine what really happened in a dispute, then summary judgment is like a paper trial, an opportunity for the judge to look at the record and assess the merits of the case. Summary judgment serves a gatekeeping function, determining whether the case should proceed to trial. Facts are the currency of litigation, and summary judgment asks whether there are facts in dispute. If there are, then they will be sorted out at trial. If there aren't contested facts, then there's no need for a full-blown trial. Why waste everyone's time if there's nothing left to figure out?

In Dawn Dawson's case, the court granted Bumble & Bumble's motion for summary judgment.[11] After looking over the record, the court concluded that neither her sex nor sexual orientation claim could stand. The problem for Dawson was that her claims were too similar. They didn't just relate to each other, but were one and the same. And this was a problem because, under Title VII of the Civil Rights Act, sex is protected but sexual orientation is not. The court concluded that Dawson's sex claim was really just a sexual orientation claim in disguise, an attempt to create statutory protection where none exists. This was *bootstrapping*,[12] and the court was having none of it. As the court saw it, there was no call for a trial. It had all the facts it needed to reach its decision. Whatever happened to Dawn Dawson at Bumble & Bumble, civil rights law wouldn't get involved.

Why not? Why didn't Dawn Dawson get her day in court?

The answer, it turns out, is that civil rights law couldn't make sense of her identity. A *woman*, a *gay* woman, a *masculine gay woman*—Dawn Dawson was, at once, too many things. She couldn't fit herself into the right box.

Civil rights law is like geometry. It deals in shapes and boundaries. It draws lines. It looks for similarities. From top to bottom, civil rights law is nothing more than a rigid system of boxes. To find shelter in the law, victims of discrimination must fit themselves into a box. The boxes are discrete and defined, fixed and un-bending. Each box houses a trait, and the existence of the box means that the trait receives protection against discrimination. The name of the game in civil rights is to anchor yourself to a box, to demonstrate that the discrimination you faced was because of a protected trait. If you can't do this—if you can't fit into one of the boxes—you have no claim. Most discrimination falls outside the reach of the law. Civil rights is a remarkably narrow enterprise.

This is by design, actually. Civil rights law restricts freedom of choice. Employers want to control their businesses as they see fit. They want to decide whom to hire and fire, how to structure their workplace, without oversight from the state. By injecting itself into workplace decision-making, civil rights law gives the state a say in how private organizations operate. Most people are at least somewhat uncomfortable with this idea. We like markets to function with limited interventions. We like the private sector to innovate. We don't want the government to get in the way.

This is why the law only sets aside a handful of traits for spe-cial protection. All forms of discrimination are bad, but the protected forms are especially problematic. These traits are

culturally salient. Often highly visible traits, they trigger deeply
held stereotypes and prejudices. Yet they bear no real relation to a
person's worth. That a person is black or female or Jewish tells me
nothing about how the person will perform at work. Civil rights
law serves to unclog the system, to rid our interactions of bias. If
we're distracted by race, take race off the table. If we can't get past
religion, take religion out of the equation. If we're dogged about
combating discrimination, civil rights law will, in time, teach us
how to be better people.

The theory is admirable, even inspiring. But things get tricky
in practice. Take the case of Beatrice Shaw.[13] A clerical worker
for a credit collection company, Shaw suffered from intermit-
tent bouts of severe body odor. Things would get so bad that her
coworkers would complain. She said it was due to a medical condition, but her doctor couldn't find a medical cause for her situation. When complaints would come in, Shaw's supervisor would
send her home early to take care of the issue. This was humili-
ating for Shaw, causing her considerable emotional distress.

Shaw sued her employer, alleging disability discrimination.
I know what you're thinking. Body odor, disability—it doesn't
add up. The basic idea was that her body odor was a medical condition that interfered with her ability to do her job. More accu-
rately, it impaired her coworkers' ability to do their jobs. At trial,
however, Shaw failed to present evidence that her body odor was
a medical condition and, as a result, the jury rejected her claim.
It found that she was not disabled in the legal sense of the term.[14]

As strange as it may seem, body odor is a great example to
tease out how boxes work in civil rights law. Remember that each
box represents an identity trait. To state an actionable claim, a
claimant must fit into one of the boxes. There is no box for body

odor. As a society, we may dislike and harbor ill feelings toward people with bad body odor, but Congress hasn't seen fit—yet?—to pass a law outlawing body odor discrimination. So Shaw had to state her claim at a greater level of generality. She chose to describe her case in terms of disability. Though she was ultimately unable to prove it, she believed that her condition was medical in nature. Her hope was that her employer—and, more importantly, her coworkers—would find a means to accommodate her body odor, just as it (and they) would any another medical condition that impaired one's ability to work. Nor should we blame Shaw for employing this strategy. She felt like she had been the victim of discrimination, and this was the only path to recovery. Justice means squeezing yourself into a box.

And sometimes body odor discrimination is more than just body odor discrimination. The San Diego International Airport judges taxi drivers according to a checklist of fifty-two criteria. Drivers get a grade: pass, fail, or needs fixing. There are criteria you'd expect to see, such as proof of insurance, safe tires, and functioning brakes, for example. And others you might not, like body odor. If a taxi driver is going to pick up passengers at the airport, the driver must pass the smell test—an honest-to-goodness smell test. A spokeswoman for the San Diego Regional Airport Authority told the Associated Press, "Taxi Drivers are often the first impression that travelers receive when arriving in San Diego, and we want to encourage a positive experience."[15] Drivers believe there is something else going on.

Most of the taxi drivers in San Diego are immigrants. And a significant chunk of them come from East Africa. Leaders of the taxi worker union said that the rule is based on a widely known stereotype that foreign-born taxi drivers smell bad.

Surely you've come across this stereotype before. It's a staple of
American comedy. Take Jerry Seinfeld's famous bit about cabbies
in New York City.[16] "The cabbies and the B.O.," he begins. "What is
with the B.O. and these guys? How long are these shifts? Can we get
this man a ten-minute break for a shower? You're in the back and
it's coming through the glass. You're just going: 'What in the . . .?'"

Eventually, Seinfeld turns to what it takes to become a cab
driver: "I think all you need is a face. This seems to be their big
qualification. No blank heads are allowed driving cabs in this
town." Which brings him to the payoff

> Also helps to have a name with like eight consonants in a
> row. Did you ever see some of the letters in these names?
> What is the "O" with the line through it, by the way? What
> planet is that from? You need a chart of the elements if you
> wanna report the guy. "Yes, officer, his name was Amal and
> then the symbol for Boron."

It's not that they're smelly; it's that they're foreign and smelly,
funny names and all.

Perhaps the San Diego International Airport's policy is not so
much about body odor but national origin. A protected trait, civil
rights law says that we cannot treat people differently simply because they hail from a particular country or part of the world.
Boxes can be deceiving. Sometimes one form of discrimination
manifests as another kind of discrimination.

Dawn Dawson faced an uphill battle from the outset. Lesbian and
gay plaintiffs have never really found their footing in civil rights
law. The vast majority of courts agree that sexual orientation is

not a protected trait under Title VII of the Civil Rights Act.[17] When the statute says "sex," it means men and women, masculinity and femininity, but not sexual orientation.

The distinction between sex and sexual orientation is fuzzy at best. After all, in our culture, sexual orientation is defined according to sex. According to conventional thinking, straight people are sexually attracted to people who are a different sex than themselves, gay people are sexually attracted to people who are the same sex as themselves, and bisexuals go both ways. Sexual orientation is, in this sense, all about sex.

Of course, it doesn't have to be this way. We could define sexuality along any number of axes. In her classic book *The Epistemology of the Closet*, critical theorist Eve Sedgewick explores some possibilities.[18] We could define it by how much sex we have (a lot, a little), or through a connection with someone (in a relationship, outside a relationship), or whether sex follows a pattern (scripted) or goes in different directions (spontaneous). I'd add to the list the time of day we like to have sex (morning, night), or the character of sex (sweet, rough). I once heard an academic say her sexual orientation was graduate student. Sex isn't the only way of thinking about sexuality, but it is the way we tend to think of it, which means that, in a case like Dawn Dawson's, civil rights law has to wade into murky waters where sex and sexual orientation intersect.

Consider Dawson's allegations against Bumble & Bumble.[19] One coworker said that Dawson wore her sexuality like a costume. Another said that she needed to have sex with a guy. They called her "Donald" and "dyke." And they said she acted too much like a man and not enough like a woman. The court's job was to disentangle these allegations, to assign each to its appropriate box. Is telling someone she wears her sexuality like a costume evidence of sex discrimination or sexual orientation discrimination? What about "dyke?" Having sex with a guy?

I think the best way to approach a case like this is to resist the urge to disentangle. New discrimination is messy, and some messes are too hard to clean. Assuming her allegations are true, the most likely story is that Dawson's coworkers were reacting to both her sex and sexual orientation, at the same time, in concert. They weren't thinking in terms of discrete boxes. Dawson's identity spans many boxes. Like all of us, she is many things all at once.

Civil rights law has always struggled with overlapping identity traits. Take a classic example. In *DeGraffenreid v. General Motors*,[20] five African American women challenged the carmaker's seniority system, which, the women argued, discriminated against black women. For most of its history, the company simply did not hire black women. That policy changed in 1964 with the passage of the Civil Rights Act. But a recession hit in the 1970s, and the company had to make layoffs. Under the company's "last hired-first fired" policy in place at the time, all the black women hired after 1964 were let go. They simply didn't have enough time in to survive the cutbacks. The plaintiffs argued that the policy perpetuated General Motors' (GM) past discrimination against black women.

This is an example of what scholars call intersectionality discrimination.[21] The idea is that some outsiders face discrimination based on overlapping traits. Rather than face bias as a woman or as a person of color, she faces bias specifically as a woman of color. Her experience is different from that of a black man or a white woman. For the plaintiffs in *DeGraffenreid*, it was not enough that they were black, nor was it enough that they were women. What mattered was that, as black women in particular, they had less of a chance to survive the layoffs.

Though it is widely accepted in the halls of academia, intersectionality theory has never really taken root in civil rights law. Courts can't reconcile the theory with the law's system of boxes. In *DeGraffenreid*, the trial court made quick work of the plaintiffs' claim. As the court saw things, the plaintiffs were trying to combine two claims—race and sex—to create a "special sub-category," a "new super-remedy which would give them relief beyond what the drafters of the relevant statutes intended."[22] The court insisted on treating their race and sex claims separately, and it rejected both. Their sex discrimination claims failed because there was evidence that GM did in fact hire women before 1964. It just happened that they were all white. But that didn't matter to the court. In light of this evidence, plaintiffs could not argue that GM engaged in discrimination against women.

Regarding the race claim, the court decided not to touch it. There was a similar race discrimination case against GM before a different judge, so the court dismissed the plaintiffs' claim so they could join the other case. Yet that didn't prevent the court from damning their theory of discrimination. "The legislative history surrounding Title VII does not indicate that the goal of the statute was to create a new classification of 'black women' who would have greater standing than, for example, a black male," the court said.[23] But it didn't stop there. It added these words of caution: "The prospect of the creation of new classes of protected minorities, governed only by mathematical principles of permutation and combination, clearly raises the prospect of opening the hackneyed Pandora's box."[24]

Nor can we dismiss this reasoning just because it comes from an earlier, less enlightened time. The court in Dawn Dawson's case employed the exact same thinking. Dawson alleged that she faced discrimination as a masculine lesbian, a hybrid claim involving elements of sex and sexual orientation discrimination. Like in *DeGraffenreid*, the court treated the two components of her claim separately, and it likewise rejected both. Like the women in *DeGraffenreid*, Dawn Dawson found herself shut out of civil rights law not because she couldn't fit into a box, but because she fit into too many boxes.

There are only two surviving photos of Frédéric Chopin, the great Polish composer, and he is scowling in both of them. Was Chopin an unhappy man? Surely not all the time. Maybe he was having a bad day. Maybe he hated having his photo taken. Maybe he disliked the photographer. Or maybe he was, in fact, a sour guy. A snapshot can't fully capture who a person really is.

Though I'm not a devoted listener of classical music, I like Chopin a lot. It is the perfect background music, seeping into my head as I work or putter around the house. I like to think that Chopin co-authored every paper I wrote in college. So I was pleasantly surprised when Chopin's scowl popped up in my car.

I was parked in the garage at work, car still running, listening to Radiolab on my cell phone. The episode was about translation—more specifically, about how words create meaning. The hosts were interviewing Professor Douglas Hofstadter, a cognitive scientist at Indiana University, Bloomington. Hofstadter is as famous as a professor gets, but the conversation wasn't about his academic work. Instead, it was about his obsession with translating an obscure French poem into English, an obsession that resulted in a book spanning more than eight hundred pages.[25] The conversation meanders, but it ultimately lands on the ethics of translation. What does the translator owe the poet? Must the translator cling to the letter of the poem, or is there room to tinker? Do we need to understand who the poet really was in order to appreciate the poem?

Jad Abumrad, one of the co-hosts of the show, asks Hofstadter this question: "Isn't the expectation that you, as a translator, are giving me him? This man is lost to time and now suddenly I get to experience him."[26]

Hofstadter pushes back against the idea that there is one essence of the poem or the poet. He argues that every translation, even if it departs from the literal language or meaning or structure of the poem, teaches us something about who the poet was. By way of analogy, he brings up Chopin and his scowl:

> What did Frédéric Chopin really look like? What was his smile like? You know, you look at a photograph of Chopin and you say 'This is what Chopin looked like.' Well, no, Chopin looked like many things. Even the very day that that photograph was taken, he had thousands of different expressions on his face. But then, what about a year earlier, or ten years earlier? I mean, knowing Chopin is a very complex thing. It's not one thing; it's millions of different things that are united by analogy into something we refer to as one thing.[27]

The exchange was captivating, but what really got me was the way Abumrad, the co-host, says by way of summarizing Hofstadter's argument. "Any person is a kind of universe," he says. "They're too big to comprehend in their entirety."[28]

Civil rights law has a translation problem. The entire antidiscrimination enterprise rests on the belief that a snapshot is a reliable indication of who a person is. When we are put into a box, we become a refraction of ourselves, a tiny piece of a larger puzzle. Civil rights law flattens identity, reducing people to a single trait. Dawn Dawson is more than her sexuality, just as Chopin is more than his scowl.

The box is the problem. We can do better.

Nathaniel Burrage drove a truck for FedEx, based out of the company's Youngstown, Ohio terminal.[29] During his years in Youngstown, Burrage had a rough time with his coworkers. They called him "Mexican" and "cheap labor."[30] They said "Andale, andale" and "Arriba, arriba" to him as he drove a forklift. They pelted him with paperclips and chalk. One time, coworkers alerted him to some demeaning graffiti on a trailer. Was it true, they wanted to know, that Mexicans were "proof that American Indians had sex with buffalos?"

Burrage reported the harassment, but his complaints fell on deaf ears. Not surprisingly, of course, as his supervisors also took part in the teasing. Not only did they call him "Mexican" and "cheap labor," too, but they laughed at him when he objected to the name-calling, and they continued to call him names. Over time, Burrage began to lose interest in his work. The teasing wore him down. He was embarrassed, ashamed. When he had finally had enough, Burrage secured a transfer to a nearby terminal.

The thing is that Nathaniel Burrage is not Mexican. Yes, his skin is brown, but he self-identifies as black, the child of a black father and a white mother. His coworkers simply got his identity wrong. And he was particularly sensitive about it, as a former girlfriend once asked him to pretend to be Mexican when he met her family. Apparently, she didn't think her family would accept him if they knew he was black.[31]

Burrage brought a lawsuit against FedEx, charging that he suffered harassment on the basis of his race. Which raises a tricky question: Is there such a thing as discrimination by mistake?

Not according to the court. In order to bring a discrimination claim, the court concluded, a claimant must actually belong to the disfavored group in question. Burrage wasn't actually Mexican, so he didn't have a claim against FedEx. That he identified as black wasn't enough. The discrimination and harassment had to be directed at his actual race. Offensive stereotypes about Latinos, no matter how harmful and destructive to Burrage's working conditions, don't cut it.

These mistaken identity cases show up from time to time and the results are discouraging, as courts deem actual group membership to be essential.[32] It is not enough that the claimant fit in a box; the claimant must fit in the correct box. There is, however, one arena in which mistaken identity does not spoil a discrimination claim: disability law.

The Americans with Disabilities Act (ADA) has what's called a "regarded as" provision.[33] It opens up the law to nondisabled people who face discrimination by mistake. Consider an example.[34] Lieutenant James Darcy, a narcotics officer with the New York City Police Department, was transferred from the Queens Narcotics division, a prestigious assignment, to the Bronx Transit division, a less prestigious assignment. Darcy believed that his transfer was based on a mistake about his identity. Specifically, his superiors believed—wrongly, as it turned out— that Darcy was an alcoholic. Darcy didn't actually need to be an alcoholic; it was enough that his employer though he was an alcoholic.

Imagine the possibilities. Why not let Nathaniel Burrage bring a regarded-as-Mexican claim? Why restrict mistaken identity claims to the disability arena?

Remember that civil rights law is supposed to be narrow. It picks and chooses. After all, a box can only hold so much. Some forms of discrimination, however loathsome, however bad for society, cannot find refuge in civil rights law. A case like Nathaniel Burrage's threatens to undermine the whole enterprise. That's the thing about boxes: They only work if they have defined boundaries. The box derives its power by being exclusive. Some cases just don't fit.

In 1964, when the Civil Rights Act came into being, the box made sense. When formal segregation was the norm, a single trait could determine a person's lot in life. The box was the best means to combat old discrimination. And it did, transforming civic life, creating new opportunities for various populations that had long been shut out of the American Dream. In our current environment, however, the box feels like a relic. New discrimination is not like old discrimination. Whereas old discrimination was stark, new discrimination is blurry. Whereas old discrimination was blatant, new discrimination is subtle. Whereas old discrimination was pervasive, new discrimination is local.

Yesterday's tools aren't equipped to solve today's problems. The box is an outmoded technology. We need a new vision of civil rights.

Create more boxes. That's the most common response to a case like Dawn Dawson's. If Dawson stumbled because of the way the law treats sexual orientation, fix the way the law treats sexual orientation. Amend the statute. Pass a new law. Change the landscape.

Easier said than done. Advocates for gay equality have been trying to get such a law passed since 1974, when Representative Bella Abzug, a Democratic congresswoman from New York, proposed the "Equality Act."[35] The bill would have expanded the Civil Rights Act to protect marital status and sexual orientation. The bill never made it out of committee, and every subsequent attempt to pass such legislation since has likewise failed. The closest a bill of this kind has ever come to passing was in 2013, when the Employment Non-Discrimination Act (ENDA) passed the Senate but died in the House.[36] The sticking point for opponents was whether the bill sufficiently exempts religious institutions from the reach of the statute.[37]

It is exceptionally hard to amend civil rights statutes, even more so if the amendment aims to broaden the reach of the law to protect new classes of people. Politics stand in the way. Legislatures are reactive bodies, more likely to respond to change than initiate it on their own. Lawmaking is an exercise in cooperation, a delicate balance of give and take. Legislators must answer to their constituents, and a good chunk of the country remains opposed to gay rights. No matter how far we've come in the fight for marriage equality, antidiscrimination protection is still out of reach.

Yet there is another wrinkle to Dawson's case. Recall that Dawson sued Bumble & Bumble under two distinct statutes. Her sex discrimination claim arose under the Civil Rights Act, while her sexual orientation claim was a creature of New York state law. In the universe of her lawsuit, sexual orientation was a protected trait. She didn't need an Equality Act or ENDA. She was protected. She had checked all the right boxes.

And yet she still lost. Never forget that antidiscrimination protection is not like a vaccine; it will not eradicate discrimination. At its most, antidiscrimination protection provides a pathway to relief. Think of it this way: Did the Civil Rights Act of 1964 do away with race discrimination? Of course it didn't. Race discrimination persists as a social phenomenon. In the years since the Civil Rights Act became law, race discrimination has evolved, not disappeared. Law is a tool of change, not a marker of change in and of itself. Yes, we must expand the reach of the law. Yes, we must make the law more accessible to outsiders. But the question is whether adding more boxes is the best means to achieve these goals.

I don't believe it is. Eventually, we will have to confront the limitations of our current system for righting wrongs. Adding more boxes is not a long-term solution. There will always be another trait that needs protecting, another outsider in search of legal relief. The universe of wrongs is limitless. There will never be enough boxes.

Michael was a student in my sex discrimination seminar. An older student, he had come back to law school after working for a few years. Normally, work experience, even just a year in the real world, benefits law students immensely. They learn what it's like to have a boss, to follow instructions, to rely on others and have others rely on you. They return to school more professionals than students, determined to make the most of a second stab at school.

But Michael (not his real name) was missing deadlines. In addition to having him in my class, we were also working together on an independent study. He was writing a paper and I was serving as his advisor. Advisor isn't really the right word for it, however. While I was counseling him on his research and writing, I was also his examiner. Ultimately, I would have to give him a grade. So I was concerned that things weren't going well.

When it comes to grades, I'm a softy. I talk a big game, making threats about how harsh my grades will be, in the hope that I will scare my students into doing their best. And it usually works. When I succeed as a teacher, it's because I can connect with my students, make them understand that I want them to thrive in their careers. I'm a better cheerleader than disciplinarian. Other teachers can pull off being a hardass without alienating their students. I can't.

Michael is the only student I have ever failed. He didn't turn in a bunch of assignments. Even worse, he wasn't staying in touch. Every time a deadline passed without hearing from him, I would send him a message, checking in. Where is your work? What's going on? I'd urge him to meet with me. In my experience, students do not learn well over email. This is true of the millennials who fill the halls of law schools today. They, too, do better work when they have to explain things to your face. So Michael and I would meet in person. He had his excuses, to be sure, but I never really cared about that. I was worried about him. I just wanted him to make progress. I didn't want this to be a thing.

When he missed another important deadline, my patience was up. We met and I made it clear: Get me your draft by a certain date, otherwise you fail. The due date came and went, with no word from Michael. So I failed him.

It must have been a jolt. I heard from him almost immediately. He had a draft; it just needed a little bit of work but he could get it to me soon. This was his last semester. He was scheduled to graduate, to take the bar exam, to start a job. Now the independent study was standing in the way. Without these credits, he couldn't graduate. But I wouldn't budge. I just couldn't. I've had students who were wisecracks, students who were lazy. I've had students who were condescending, students who were disruptive. But I've never had a student who had no regard for my authority. It was unprofessional, a gross violation of the teacher-student relationship. I couldn't let it stand. Being a softy is one thing. This was someone else.

He came to see me, and it was brutal. He was angry, of course, and hurt. He thought I was being unfair. Then he accused me of discrimination. He said he couldn't help but think that I failed him because he is gay. I kicked him out of my office. Years later, I still feel bad about that. I wish I handled it better. I wish I kept the conversation going. I didn't fail him because he is gay. I failed him because he didn't do the work and, more importantly, because he lied about it. He simply didn't communicate with me. There were so many points along the way where he could have asked for help, where I could have thrown him a lifeline. But he didn't speak up. When he finally did, it was too late.

In the end, Michael averted disaster. Another faculty member took him on and, together, they hammered out the paper. He graduated and took the bar. I don't know what he's up to now. But his story is never far from my mind. It's a story about boxes, about how we locked into ideas about each other, causing us to view the same interaction in starkly different terms. It is a story about the limits of conversation, what happens when people who need to communicate can't. And it is a story about failure, both his and mine.

Lacey Schwartz was white before she was black.[38] Raised in the largely white enclave of Woodstock, New York, Schwartz grew up an only child in a typical Jewish home. Schwartz's parents, Robert and Peggy, told her that her skin color was the product of a distant relative on Robert's side of the family, a Sicilian great-great-grandfather with a dark complexion. Some Jews do indeed have dark skin, especially Sephardic Jews who trace their lineage to the Iberian Peninsula. So it was reasonable for her to accept the explanation. Besides, kids don't often question their parents about these sorts of things. It didn't matter that, at her Bat Mitzvah, a member of her congregation congratulated Schwartz for being an Ethiopian Jew.[39] She was white. Her parents said so.

Then she went to college. After she was accepted into Georgetown University, she received an introductory note from the black student group on campus. Having seen Schwartz's photograph from her admissions materials, the group reached out to encourage her to join the organization. They saw what Schwartz hadn't been able to see.[40]

Schwartz confronted her mother, who revealed the truth. Peggy had an extramarital affair with a friend of the family, and that man was Schwartz's birth father. And he was black. Schwartz and the swarthy Sicilian weren't blood relatives after all.

Today, Schwartz identifies as biracial. She tells her story in the documentary "Little White Lie." In it, she says that it never occurred to her that she was passing. "I wasn't pretending to be something I wasn't. I actually grew up believing that I was white."[41]

In the previous chapter, we talked about identity conversions, when people take steps to change their identity. Krystal Etsitty, the bus driver in Utah, embarked on a journey to become a woman. Martin, the character in Jess Row's novel, underwent a series of surgeries to make himself a black man. Lacey Schwartz's story is different. She is not a racial convert. Her race didn't change. It was her sense of self that changed.

Our bodies do not define us. We are more than just a collection of traits. Identity is as much about how we perceive ourselves as it is about how others see us. Consider the fracture within the deaf community over cochlear implants. For some deaf people, cochlear implants are a revolutionary technology, a scientific solution to a debilitating impairment. Other deaf people, by contrast, view cochlear implants as a means of abandoning deaf culture. One man's progress is another man's retreat.

The debate over cochlear implants is a debate about authenticity. It is a debate about what it means to be a real deaf person. Every community has its own version of this battle. Within the gay community, for example, marriage became a source of considerable tension. Some gay people wanted the right to marry because they wanted to be treated like straight people. Other gay people saw marriage as a significant step backward for gay liberation. We see a similar struggle within immigrant communities over whether to speak English or retain their native tongue. For transgender people, the question of whether to go stealth—the transgender term for being in the closet—is as fraught as it is inevitable. Who is blacker, the person who listens to hip-hop or the person who rocks out to classic country music? Is the Jew who doesn't go to synagogue still a Jew?

Authenticity comes from within. The search for identity is about self-discovery, about finding one's place in the world. How a person feels about herself, about who she is and where she belongs in the world, matters just as much as the traits she wears on her body, sometimes even more so.

That was certainly the case for Lacey Schwartz. With time, she grew into her skin. And her name began to make a little more sense, too. A common Jewish surname, Schwartz is the German word for black. Lacey Schwartz's search for identity freed her from a secret life she didn't even know she had been living, enabling her to be herself, to live a life that felt right to her.

So what do we do? How to do we get beyond the box? Once again, religious discrimination offers a blueprint for a new civil rights.

Religious discrimination law shows us how to build an antidiscrimination system that takes people on their own terms and lets them be themselves. It shows us that the box is not essential to the work of righting wrongs. And it shows us that difference has a place in the law. Moving forward does not require forgetting our past. Civil rights law has done so much good, brought about so much change, made so many lives better. But it can do more. The box is the problem. We can do better.

In 2001, while her lawsuit was still in progress, Dawn Dawson gave an interview to the group GenderPac, an LGBT rights organization based in Washington, D.C.[42] The interview begins with some background about the lawsuit. She had been cutting hair already, but she moved to Bumble & Bumble because she wanted to make more money for her family. The problems started soon thereafter. "There were all these jokes about my being butch,"[43] she said. "And it's like when you start to get a little funny feeling in your stomach, when someone starts teasing you on the playground, and then it starts to hurt, and finally you realize it's getting out of hand and you can't stop it."[44]

Faced with a tough situation at work, Dawson did what most people do: She tried to ignore it. She is a good sport; she can take a joke. She wanted to do right by her family. So she made the decision to stick it out and make the best of a difficult situation. Unfortunately, she didn't realize her job was at stake until it was too late. She was reprimanded for shaving the sides of her head. It was too severe, too much of a military look. This was when a superior told her that she couldn't get a job outside New York because she would scare people. Dawson was working twelve to thirteen hours a day, six days a week, for minimum wage. It was hard work, and it wasn't working out.

Then she was fired. The thing that hurt her most about the firing was that the woman who fired Dawson is transgender. "I know it may sound silly," Dawson said, "but coming from her, it hurt more."[45] Dawson was expecting some level of kinship. Outsiders must stick together, she thought, especially a gay woman and transgender woman. But the politics of the place were messy. The salon had fired gay people before. "They wanted gay people," Dawson said, "but gay people who were passably gay. Anyone who rode the line was fired."[46]

Why did she sue the salon? It wasn't about money or getting her job back. Lawyers care about liability and remedies. For litigants, however, lawsuits are more personal. She pursued the case because she wanted to stand up for herself. Sometimes a lawsuit is necessary to remind the world that outsiders are people, too, that they have families and relationships, feelings and fears, that they are as complicated and special as the next person. Sometimes it takes a lawsuit to show that every person's experience matters. "It's about equality for all of us," Dawson said to conclude the interview.[47]

And she's right about that. Identity is only half the battle. We still have to contend with equality.

PART TWO

Equality

4
—

Visions of Equality

In the world of sports, the PGA Tour is the pinnacle of golf. Professional golfers traverse the globe, playing tournaments on the world's finest courses. Spectators gather at the greens and line the fairways, while millions of fans watch from their couches at home. Fame and fortune are on the line. The winners become household names, earn lucrative endorsement deals, and remake the sport in their image. The competition is fierce and the play is unparalleled. Lots of people play golf, but very few have the talent to play on the tour.

Casey Martin is one of the few.[1] As a junior player, Martin won seventeen tournaments in his home state of Oregon, all before his fifteenth birthday. He won the Oregon state championship during his senior year of high school. In college, he helped guide the Stanford men's team to the National Collegiate Athletic Association (NCAA) championship. He also won the Sahalee Players Championship, a major amateur tournament, in 1993. An elite player, Martin had what it takes to succeed at the highest level of the sport.

Provided he could walk the course. PGA rules prohibit the use of golf carts in competition. To get his tour card, Martin needed to survive a three-stage qualifying tournament, what the pros call Q-School, and he had to do it on foot.[2] The problem was that Martin can't walk long distances. He suffers from Klippel–Trénaunay syndrome, a rare congenital condition that prevents blood vessels from forming properly. As a result of this condition, Martin's right leg is weak—so weak, in fact, that if he walked the course, he risked breaking his tibia so badly that it would have to be amputated. Hemorrhaging and blood clots were also possible. Severe pain and fatigue were certain. That other elite golfers could walk the course didn't matter. For Martin, walking the course was not an option. He wanted to play professionally, and the walking rule was standing in his way.

According to the PGA, the purpose of the no-cart rule is to introduce fatigue into the game.[3] Over the course of a tournament, players walk significant distances, something like five miles for every eighteen holes. Top competitors in a major tournament play seventy-two holes over four days. That's the better part of a marathon, and they do it week after week when the tour is in full swing. So, yes, fatigue becomes a factor.

Yet fatigue is a part of Martin's daily life, not just his golf game. When he was in college, Martin applied to the Pac 10 and the NCAA for a waiver of their rules requiring players to walk and carry their own clubs. Both organizations approved the waiver, allowing Martin to use a cart during tournament play.[4]

The professional tour was a different story. Although players could use carts during the first two rounds of Q-School, everyone had to walk for the final round. Martin made a formal request to use a cart during the third round. He supported the request with extensive medical documentation. The PGA Tour refused to waive the walking rule.[5]

So Martin sued the PGA Tour, alleging disability discrimination. He argued that the walking rule amounted to a denial of equality.

On the first day of my sex discrimination course, I ask my students to do a brainstorming exercise. Discrimination is one of those subjects where students come into a class with well-formed beliefs. So it is useful to start out by getting a sense of the room, to see who and what we're dealing with. This isn't something I have to do in my property law course. Discrimination is special that way. Heated conversations and hurt feelings are part of the course. Mine is one of the few courses in the curriculum that forces students to confront their own, as well as their classmates', ideas about justice.

The exercise is simple. I ask them to word associate with a few key terms in the field—sex, discrimination, equality, among others. We do one term at a time. They jot down their thoughts, and then we go around the room discussing their answers. After a few of them take a turn, the discussion snowballs. They build on each other's answers. They disagree. They refer back to earlier comments. They strain to resolve inconsistencies. Since it's the beginning of the semester, they make a concerted effort to be constructive and not offend one another. It's a great way to start a conversation about civil rights.

And it's revealing. Year in, year out, no matter the makeup of the class, the results are always the same. They have strong opinions about what sex means. They waffle a bit over what discrimination means. But they find equality vexing. While they feel like they know what equality is, they struggle to put their understanding into words. In this respect, equality is a little like obscenity: We know it when we see it.[6]

My students' trouble with equality is understandable. Although it is the cornerstone of American civil rights law, equality is an elusive concept. Consider, for example, a recent book on comparative antidiscrimination law, a law school casebook that tracks equality law across the globe. In its introduction, the book opens with a brief primer on what equality might mean. "Ideas and applications of equality span a conceptual range that is impossible to capture completely here," the book's editors explain.[7] Rather than stop there, however, the editors offer a list of different ways of thinking about equality. Among them are equal opportunity, accommodation, respect, and dignity, as well as subordination, human rights, and civil rights. In all, the list has thirty-four entries. And the list is not meant to be exhaustive. There is no better reminder that there is no one way to do equality.

As an abstract idea, equality does not have much force on its own. What does it mean to treat people equally? The answer, it turns out, depends on identity. In civil rights law and policy, equality is best understood as a theory of identity. Which identities matter, which don't, and when do we make that call? Say the owner of a car dealership wants to hire a new member of its sales staff. This is a situation where sex does not matter, where sex should not factor into the decision-making process. Things would be altogether different in a casting situation. Say a producer is casting the lead actress in a romantic comedy. In this situation, sex is an essential part of the gig, what the law calls a "bona fide occupational qualification," or BFOQ.[8] Because the script calls for a woman, the producer does not have to consider men for the role.

Discrimination law devotes a significant amount of time and attention to the question of whether sex—or another identity trait—is a necessary component of a given job. Can a prison require guards to be same sex as the inmates?[9] What about nurses and their patients?[10] Can the restaurant chain Hooters refuse to hire men as servers?[11] Can a nightclub?[12] Is it necessary that the maintenance staff at a synagogue be Jewish?[13] Can an airline force its pilots to retire once they reach retirement age?[14]

These questions require a vision of equality. To answer them, we have to decide where and when identity matters. We have to decide, in other words, what we want civil rights law to achieve. This chapter distinguishes between two visions of equality—sameness and difference. Sameness is the more dominant of the two, undergirding much of civil rights law as we know it. Difference, by contrast, occupies a smaller share of the landscape. The goal of this chapter is to make the case for difference.

In its broadest sweep, this book is an ode to difference. Being different is universal. We are all outsiders. We stand out. We don't fit in. We conceal our true selves. Difference cuts across groups, binding us to each other. Difference unites us, instilling in us a sense of common humanity. We all want to be ourselves fully, to live authentic lives. Civil rights law can make this possible.

A trial is a spectacle. There are speeches, interviews, secret meetings between the parties. Lawyers object. The judge, who is wearing a costume, makes rulings. The whole thing takes place in public, witnessed by voluntary spectators in the gallery, as well as reluctant spectators in the jury box. Some trials make waves in the media. Every now and then a trial becomes a national sensation.

Casey Martin's trial wasn't a sensation, but it had its moments. In its attempt to justify the walking rule, the PGA Tour arranged for giants of the golf world to testify on the Tour's behalf. Jack Nicklaus, Arnold Palmer, and Ken Venturi—three of the winningest golfers of all time—testified about the role of fatigue in professional golf. Palmer explained that fatigue can cause a golfer to lose a stroke, which can be the difference between winning and losing a tournament. "As I said, I've lost a few national opens by one stroke," he said.[15] Nicklaus, too, emphasized the effect of fatigue. "Well, in my opinion, physical fitness and fatigue are part of the game of golf," he said.[16] And Venturi laid it out succinctly: "It will influence your game. It will influence your shot-making. It will influence your decisions."[17]

Though they didn't say so explicitly, the greats were against allowing Martin to use a golf cart. If everyone else has to walk, the cart would give Martin an unfair advantage over his competitors. As they tire, he will remain fresh.

The PGA Tour's argument was based on the idea that it had to maintain a level playing field. If it treats one player differently, the rest of the players suffer as a result. This is an equality argument based on sameness.

Equality as sameness holds that, despite our differences, people are fundamentally the same. We may look different, come from different backgrounds, and believe different things, but these differences should not define who we are. The traits we wear on our bodies seem important but shouldn't be. When we peel back people's outer layer, everyone looks the same. Within the universe of sameness, to treat people equally is to ignore what makes them different.

In civil rights law and policy, equality as sameness is often talked about in terms of blindness. In his celebrated book *Prejudicial Appearances*, law professor Robert Post argues that there is a logic underlying American civil rights law, and this logic depends on blindness.[18] "Blindness," he says, "renders forbidden characteristics invisible; it requires employers to base their judgments instead on the deeper and more fundamental ground of 'individual merit' or 'intrinsic worth.'"[19] Deployed in this context, blindness is not an impairment, but a choice. We act as if we cannot see a person's race or sex or disability. We act as if identity does not matter, in the hope that one day it won't.

For the PGA Tour, treating Casey Martin equally means ignoring his disability. Permitting him to use a cart would amount to special rights, a benefit to the other golfers' detriment. That he struggles to walk is not relevant to the issue at hand. According to the controlling rules of the game, a golfer must be able to walk the course. If Martin can't walk the course, he can't play the game.

Martin, of course, saw the matter in another light. He made an equality argument based on difference. He didn't argue that he was similarly situated to the rest of the field. Nor was his claim that the law should be blind to his identity. To the contrary, he argued that the law needed to be hyper-focused on his identity. His hope was that the tour would accommodate him, that it would, in other words, mold itself around his disability.

Equality as difference rejects the idea that people are fundamentally the same. It reasons, instead, that identity is dynamic. That two people belong to the same group does not tell us everything about them, but rather just an aspect of who they are. There is no such thing as a truly homogenous group: No two members of a group express their identity in exactly the same way. People have different wants, needs, experiences. Some of these correlate with a person's identity. Others do not. Often, the thing that makes a person stand out is integral to the person's sense of self. Difference matters. Difference is what makes us, us.

Rather than ignore it, equality as difference holds that we should embrace identity in its fullest dimensions, accepting people as we find them. This is equality in a substantive, rather than formal, sense. Writing many years ago, in the context of race discrimination, Justice Harry Blackmun said that, "in order to treat some persons equally, we must treat them differently."[20] Some people can't be treated the same as everyone else. Some identities require more care, more attention.

Casey Martin needed a golf cart. Treating Martin equally meant treating him differently. The trial court said as much. So did the appellate court. And eventually the Supreme Court, too. All three courts saw Martin's request as reasonable and necessary, something that enabled him to do what he does best. Martin's story is a classic example of how equality as difference works. Take a person on his own terms, figure out what he needs to flourish, and assess whether it is possible to accommodate him. Casey Martin wasn't like the other golfers on the Tour. And civil rights law intervened on his behalf.

Misty Copeland shouldn't be a ballerina. She came to dance late, taking her first ballet class at age thirteen, at the Boys and Girls club near her home, in San Pedro, California.[21] Nor does she look the part. Most ballerinas are impossibly thin and lithe. They have long legs and short torsos, living embodiments of the so-called "Balanchine Body," named for the heralded American chore-ographer George Balanchine. Copeland's body is a rejoinder to Balanchine. She is strong, buxom, athletic—and black.

"Most ballet companies look like an Alabama country club in 1952," says Susan Fales-Hill, a writer and patron of the American

Ballet Theatre (ABT), the country's preeminent classical ballet company.[22] Copeland joined ABT in 2007. Today she is a principal in the company, the first African American woman to have achieved that height.[23]

Copeland was recently featured in an Under Armour commercial, part of the sportswear company's "I Will What I Want" campaign.[24] In the ad, Copeland wears a sports bra and underwear, and she dances, slowly at first, then fiercely as the music quickens. In voiceover, a young girl reads a rejection letter from a ballet academy. "Dear Candidate. Thank you for your application to our ballet academy. Unfortunately, you have not been accepted." As Copeland rises onto pointe, the letter lists things that are wrong with her—her feet, Achilles tendon, turnout, torso length and bust. "You have the wrong body for ballet and, at thirteen, you are too old to be considered." The commercial doesn't mention her race, but it doesn't have to.

The letter is fiction, but the sentiment is fact: Misty Copeland is different. She frustrates our expectations about ballet, and in the best way. She represents change, an evolution of beauty in an art form that favors grace above all else.

The life of a dancer is hard. Copeland's, of course, is harder. Like all trailblazers, she carries a hefty burden on her shoulders. When she was younger, Copeland tried to cover her race. To make herself stand out less, she lightened her skin with powder. "I was painting my skin a completely different color, taking the ivory base foundation used by one of the other girls and layering it on my face and arms to lighten my skin," she writes in her memoir, *Life in Motion*.[25] Dancers often "pancake" their pointe shoes, using makeup to give the shoes a matte finish. Copeland was pancaking her race, giving herself a matte finish.

Those days are behind her. Today Misty Copeland is proud of her body and her prodigious talent, and she is trying to change the face of ballet. As Bill Whitaker, a reporter for CBS's *60 Minutes* explains, Copeland's goal is to make "ballet in America look like America, on stage and in the audience."[26]

Copeland's race is entangled with her talent. There will never be a story about her dancing that doesn't make note of her race. This comes with being first. The paradox of her success is that, every time she takes the stage, she highlights the work that still needs to be done.

Tchaikovsky's *Swan Lake* is perhaps the most famous ballet of all. It tells the story of Odette, a princess who, under an evil curse, becomes a swan. As the white swan, she falls in love with a prince, and only he can lift the curse. The evil sorcerer tries to trick the prince into marrying Odile, the black swan. The ploy backfires. The curse is lifted, but Odette dies in the process. So they can be together, the prince joins Odette in death.

A week before she was promoted to principal, Misty Copeland starred in ABT's production of *Swan Lake*. ABT followed customary practice for *Swan Lake*, with Copeland portraying both the white swan and black swan. But this was no ordinary performance. It was the first time a black woman had played the lead role at the company's home, the Metropolitan Opera House. After the ballet concluded, at the curtain call, Copeland was greeted on stage by two retired African American ballerinas, prominent dancers who helped to pave the way for Copeland.

A good children's movie is like a good college town: It has to appeal to two very different audiences at the same time. *Frozen* is a very good children's movie,[27] the Ann Arbor of Disney films. Like so many other little kids around the world, my daughter went crazy for *Frozen*. She watched it over and over again, learning the dialogue, singing the songs, becoming immersed in its world. Like so many parents around the world, I watched *Frozen* over and over again, learning the dialogue, singing the songs, getting sucked into its world.

A lot of academics see the world through their area of study. I once had a friend, a Plato scholar, who could, and usually did, relate everything to Plato. That's not normally my style. But *Frozen* is an exception. *Frozen* is about difference, identity, and authenticity. It is about what happens when we try to hide the truth about who we really are, and about coming clean and being accepted by those around us.

For the uninitiated, *Frozen* tells the story of two sisters, Elsa and Anna. They are princesses; it's a Disney movie, after all. As young children, Elsa and Anna are as close as can be. They play together and clearly love each other. Elsa has either a special talent or a curse, depending on how you look at it. She has the ability to freeze things. She can shoot ice from her hands. She can freeze water. She can even build a castle made of ice. Using Elsa's power, the girls build snowmen, throw snowballs, and sled in Elsa-made snow, until an accident derails everything.

While playing one night, Elsa accidentally hits Anna in the head with a bolt of ice. Their father, the King, rushes the family to a troll who has the magic power to save Anna. To protect Anna, the troll advises that the family to conceal the truth about Elsa's powers, even from Anna. As a result, Elsa drifts away from Anna, holing up in her room. The King insists that Elsa hide her powers. "Conceal, don't feel, don't let it show," he advises her.

The girls grow apart. Anna feels rejected—she's lost her sister and she doesn't know why. The parents eventually die at sea, and the girls have to fend for themselves. As years pass, Elsa becomes queen. At Elsa's coronation, the tension between the sisters bubbles over. Elsa's secret is revealed, as she accidentally freezes the kingdom. She runs off into the now-frozen mountains. The movie is Anna's quest to get Elsa back so she can unfreeze the world, and be her sister again.

Until the very end of the movie, Elsa is convinced that, because she's different, she belongs by herself, isolated from the rest of the world. Outsiders live a lonely existence. Being different takes its toll. The process of managing an outsider identity—be it race, religion, or magical powers—is enduring, an ongoing struggle to control information. Authenticity can be risky. This is why people stay in the closet. This is why most people come out gradually, if ever.

Although Casey Martin and Queen Elsa may not seem like they have a lot in common, their stories are fragments of a larger lesson. Both wanted to be a part of something without sacrificing what makes them special. The key difference was that Martin knew he could contribute to his desired enterprise, but Elsa had convinced herself she couldn't. This reflects a continuum of how difference is experienced. On one end are those who hide their difference—the Elsas. On the other end are those who seek acceptance for their difference—the Martins. No one is purely an Elsa or a Martin all the time. Most people flow regularly between these poles. On any given day, a person will occupy different points on the continuum. A person may be an Elsa at work but a Martin away from work. Or she may be an Elsa with her family but a Martin with her friends. The permutations are limitless.

I don't know why *Frozen* became the juggernaut it did, but I like to think it's because the movie's larger themes resonate with a kid's vision of the world. Kids are more in tune with difference, more accepting of the range of human experiences. Unburdened by social pressures, kids live authentically. They are weirdos, quite frankly, and they don't judge other kids for being weirdos, too. Somewhere along the way, kids lose their willingness to accept difference unconditionally, and it has to be taught anew. This is what civil rights law strives to do. One outsider at a time, it teaches us to treat each other better.

Take a garden-variety employment decision. Say an employer needs to make a promotion to a management position. The employer plans to promote from within the organization. There are only two viable candidates, and it's going to be tough to decide between them. With similar work experience and educational credentials, both of the candidates would do well in the position. The only material difference between them is identity: Candidate one is a male and candidate two is female.

When decision time comes, the employer promotes the man. The employer believes that the staff will respond better to the man's leadership. This is, in the end, a business decision. The employer wants what is best for the organization as a whole. The employer conveys the news, as well as the underlying rationale, to the woman. Understandably, she is upset. She lost out on the promotion, and the financial benefits that come along with it, not because of what she can do, but because of who she is. So she sues the employer, alleging discrimination. It turns out that the employer has a track record of preferring men to women, and the employer is not shy about it. What the woman sees as discrimination, the employer sees as a sound business practice.

To prove discrimination in this case, the woman needs to isolate the trait that sets her and the man apart. This is equality by algebraic equation.[28] Instead of solving for x, we're solving for sex. Cross out what they share in common—work experience, educational background, years on the job—as those things can't explain the employer's decision. What we're left with is sex. The employer did not promote candidate two because she is a woman.

Old discrimination and sameness go hand in hand. Old discrimination is about group membership and integration, and candidate two is a victim of old discrimination. She was judged solely on the grounds of her sex. She was penalized solely because belongs to an outsider group. The antidote to old discrimination is sameness. Put on blinders, ignore the trait. The way to achieve equality is to act as if difference doesn't matter and, eventually, it won't.

Now change the facts slightly. Say that the female candidate has applied for a promotion. She's put in the requisite time with the company, has all the right credentials, and has emerged as a solid contributor, an asset even. She deserves the promotion. Yet she doesn't get it. The employer explains that the management team didn't think she had matured enough on the job. Her appearance and demeanor need work. She would benefit from a new wardrobe and a little makeup, and it would help her cause if she treated those around her better. She should apply again when she's ready.

This is new discrimination, and sameness is of no help. We can't solve for x. We can't attribute this to group membership. The candidate—let's call her Ann H.—didn't look and act the part. To get the promotion, she needs to do a better job of fitting in, and fitting in is not Ann H.'s thing. Should we expect her to change who she is?

Before answering that question, change the facts once more. Instead of falling short in her appearance and demeanor, say she didn't get the promotion because, due to a birth defect, she can't talk for extended periods of time. As her voice fails her often, and she needs regular treatments—once or twice a month—that keep her away from the office for half a day. Although extensive talking is not required for the position, the management team felt that she wouldn't be able to win the support of the staff. This seems like a relatively straightforward case of disability discrimination. Here, the candidate's difference matters, so much so that the employer can't ignore it. Instead, the employer must try to accommodate it, if possible.

The disability case just feels easier than the sex case. A birth defect is beyond a person's control. She didn't choose it, so the law should do what it can to help her out. Appearance and demeanor, by contrast, are fully within a person's control. If she wanted to, she could change the way she acts and looks. The need for legal intervention is less pressing.

Civil rights law buys heavily into the distinction between being and doing. Biology is protected. Choice is not. The one exception is religion.

Religious discrimination law collapses the distinction between biology and choice. Some inherit religion from their families. Others come to theirs by choice. Some move between faiths often. Others pick and choose their beliefs. Many reject religion altogether. Religious discrimination law anticipates motion, expanding and contracting as needed to fit people's beliefs. Unlike the rest of civil rights law, religious discrimination law recognizes that identity emanates from within. We decide our faith for ourselves.

As a legal culture, we have decided to set religion apart from the rest of civil rights law. Yet there is nothing special about religion, nothing about it that requires special treatment. A devout person may recoil at this idea, and I do not mean to offend. But from the perspective of discrimination and equality, religion is no different than any other identity trait. That we treat it differently does not, in fact, make it different.

The question I asked above—Should we expect Ann H. to change who she is?—is, it turns out, the wrong question. Here's a better question: Why should anyone have to change? Maybe we're thinking about identity and equality in the wrong way. What if, instead of trying to make people fit in, we just let people be themselves? Rather than try to read minds and ferret out bias, civil rights law should redirect the inquiry. Is there space for difference? Can we accommodate the person's identity? Make the inquiry more functional. Make it address the heart of the matter. By injecting difference into the equation, civil rights law will inject difference into a sea of sameness.

Justice Scalia did not join the majority of the Court in Casey Martin's case. Along with Justice Thomas, he dissented, concluding that the PGA Tour was not required to let Martin use a golf cart. His view of the case was that the PGA Tour was not a public accommodation. The PGA Tour is not your average public course. If the Tour is a business open to the public, then that would make professional golfers customers, and that, to Justice Scalia, doesn't make a whole lot of sense. "Kafkaesque" is the way he describes it.[29]

Moreover, Justice Scalia rejects the idea that the PGA Tour should have to adopt individualized rules for each and every participant. He thinks that Martin's inability to walk means he lacks the ability to play the game as the professionals play it. And he criticizes the Court for adopting a rule that does away with difference. Which is why he ends his opinion by quoting from Kurt Vonnegut's short story *Harrison Bergeron*: "The year was 2001, and 'everybody was finally equal.' "[30]

Harrison Bergeron is a story about what would happen if equality is taken to extremes.[31] After a series of constitutional amendments, Americans must renounce natural advantages like brains, beauty, and athleticism. Ballerinas wear weights so they aren't graceful. Newscasters have speech impediments so they struggle to read the news. And smart people wear transmitters that disrupt their ability to think. As one of the characters explains, without these manmade handicaps, "pretty soon we'd be right back to the dark ages again, with everybody competing against everybody else."[32] In a truly equal society, competition is unfair. The government's job is to level the playing field, to prevent accidents of birth from determining a person's lot in life.

Justice Scalia's reference to *Harrison Bergeron* is a clever way of criticizing the Court for treating golfers as if they are all the same. But that's not what the Court was doing at all. The Court's vision of equality was based on difference, not sameness. The Americans with Disabilites Act (ADA) turns conventional equality analysis on its head. Rather than approach identity at the level of the group, the ADA treats people as individuals. There are a group of people who fall within the statute's reach, and we can consider them disabled for purposes of civil rights law. But beyond the label, they do not overlap. The question before the court isn't whether the PGA Tour must accommodate disabled golfers. It is, instead, whether it must accommodate Casey Martin. The failure to do so is not disability discrimination so much as it is Casey Martin discrimination.

The difference between group harms and individual harms is critical. Say the PGA Tour had a rule against allowing people with disabilities from playing in its tournaments. In that situation, disabled people as a group would suffer on account of the policy. Civil rights law would intervene to disrupt this practice. The remedy would be access for disabled golfers generally. But that was not what the case was about. The walking rule only became an issue because Casey Martin struggles to walk. There is a general phenomenon of discrimination against people with disabilities. It is just experienced individually.

But isn't this true for other kinds of discrimination, too? Don't racial minorities experience race discrimination individually? Isn't every case of harassment experienced uniquely? Yes, that is exactly the point. The discrimination is the same. The thing that's different is how the law responds to the discrimination. Unlike the rest of civil rights law, disability law endeavors not just to integrate outsiders but to reimagine civic spaces. Access, without more, is insufficient. Disability law demands adaptation. Ramps, elevators, interpreters, service animals, convenient parking—disability law has completely reshaped the social landscape of everyday life. The only other area of civil rights law to operate this way is religious discrimination law. Together, disability law and religious discrimination law inhabit an island of difference in a sea of sameness. The outsiders of civil rights law, disability law, and religious discrimination law, offer a roadmap for the future of civil rights.

Elizabeth Anderson's faith was important to her.[33] An office manager for a business that coordinated shipping for other companies, Anderson spent a sizeable chunk of her workday communicating with people. Her company's largest client was Microsoft, and one of Microsoft's employees had a problem with Anderson's way of communicating. He objected to her use of the phrase "Have a Blessed Day." Anderson belonged to the Christian Methodist Episcopal faith, and she regularly used the "blessed day" phrase. She said it to her coworkers. She used it to sign off on emails. And she ended her phone conversations with it. After the complaint, her employer asked Anderson to remove the phrase from any communications with Microsoft.

She didn't. For Anderson, the phrase was an expression of her faith. She firmly believed that this was a protected part of her religious life. Again, her employer asked that she not use the phrase in any communications with Microsoft. For her part, Anderson, wanted to know who specifically had a problem with it. She said she would avoid using it with those people. Neither side would budge. So Anderson sued, charging her employer with religious discrimination.

And she lost. The court concluded that the employer had offered a reasonable accommodation, namely, that she could use the phrase in conversations and emails, just not with anyone at Microsoft.[34] To reach that decision, however, the court first had to decide whether her use of the phrase was religious in nature, so as to bring within the reach of civil rights law. This was the easy part of the case. Anderson sincerely believed that the phrase was an important component of her spiritual life. She didn't use it in every conversation. She didn't claim that her church required her to say it. It was her practice, her system of belief. She set its terms and defined its limits. She was the master of her identity.

Nor is it a problem that she ultimately lost her case. Anderson got more than it seems. Her employer heard her out. It let her be herself. It didn't squelch her speech. It didn't fire her after it received the first complaint. If anything, the employer was loyal to Anderson, all the while working hard to find a solution that would satisfy everyone. We should celebrate this case. This is exactly how civil rights law should work. Rather than pit employer and employee against each other, religious discrimination law seeks common ground. Most of civil rights law operates in a winner-takes-all manner. Not so for religious discrimination law. Forcing people to communicate with each other, working to ease tensions—these are the hallmarks of religious discrimination law's accommodation mandate. Put people in a room together, let them speak their minds, let them teach each other about who they are and what they need. Through conversations like this, people become more accepting of difference.

An authoritative source on legal meaning, *Black's Law Dictionary* defines equality as follows: "The condition of possessing the same rights, privileges, and immunities, and being liable to the same duties."[35] Note how sameness is a built-in feature of equality. Equality is a condition, the condition of having the same rights. But if sameness is the cornerstone of equality, where does this leave difference?

Sameness and difference are distinct but not contradictory. If anything, they complement each other, picking up where the other leaves off. Sometimes equality turns on a comparison. Did the employer pay its male supervisors more than its female supervisors? Was a black employee punished for being late but a white employee's tardiness overlooked? In these situations, sameness is a helpful metric.

In other situations, however, comparisons aren't helpful. There was no comparison to be made in Elizabeth Anderson's case. "Have a Blessed Day" was her practice and hers alone. Sameness wasn't the issue in her case; it was whether she should receive different treatment. No need to compare anything.

The particulars of my doctrinal proposal will come later. At this point, however, it is important to be clear about the foundation upon which the proposal will rest. My argument is that difference should supplement sameness, not supplant it. Equality is not a one-size-fits-all sort of enterprise. Equality must be versatile and unstable, forever growing and changing. Equality should be personalized, tailored to fit people's needs. As we look to the future, civil rights law needs both visions of equality—sameness and difference—to address the realities of discrimination as it exists today.

Casey Martin never amounted to much as a professional golfer. Even with access to a golf cart, he didn't play well enough to make it on the tour. Eventually, he turned to coaching, landing the head coaching job for the University of Oregon's men's golf team. In his recruiting role for the team, Martin attended a 2013 U.S. Junior Amateur qualifying tournament in Oceanside, California. He planned to follow some prospective recruits as they progressed along the course. Of course he would need a cart to do that. In advance of the tournament, Martin reached out to the tournament director to arrange the accommodation.

Things worked out until the sixth hole, when the tournament director told Martin he could no longer use the cart. U.S. Golf Association (USGA) rules prohibit spectators from using carts. Because he was there in a recruiting function, Martin counted as spectator. Although the tournament director initially agreed to the accommodation, he changed his mind after receiving a call from the USGA, seeking enforcement of its no-cart policy. Martin pleaded his case, even going so far as to cite the Supreme Court's opinion in his suit against the PGA Tour.[36] But the director wouldn't budge. So Martin surrendered the cart. "I've never felt more discriminated against or unfairly taken advantage of in my entire life," Martin said at the time.[37]

This was not the first time Martin lost cart privileges after a tournament was already underway. The week before the incident in California, Martin attended a qualifier in Creswell, Oregon, again to scope out prospects for his team. After play was already underway, a tournament official likewise asked Martin to surrender his cart, citing USGA's no-cart policy. The official suggested Martin return to the clubhouse to get a single-rider scooter. When none was available, Martin left the tournament.[38]

One of the features of being different is the need to fight for your rights over and over again. Casey Martin took his fight to the Supreme Court and won. Yet he still has to convince others that his difference matters. Change doesn't happen overnight. These recent incidents are more of a smudge than a stain on his legacy. Casey Martin did indeed change the game. It wasn't his swing or his short game. It wasn't his power or his consistency. He changed the game because he stood up for himself. He demanded to be taken seriously, not in spite of, but because of his difference. He forced a conversation, and that conversation is ongoing. Equality is a process.

Accommodations

Roy Lester lives a double life.[1] By day, Lester is a bankruptcy attorney on Long Island, New York. He has three kids. He runs his own law practice. He's an accomplished triathlete and a former president of his local school board. Yet he still finds time to save lives. Roy Lester is a real-life hero. Roy Lester is a lifeguard.

Lester started lifeguarding in 1965, and he's still going strong. His longest post was at Jones Beach, a popular vacation spot at the edge of Long Island, abutting the Atlantic Ocean. For a lifeguard, Jones Beach is the big leagues. With strong currents, tall waves, and millions of swimmers every year, Jones Beach is a breeding ground for rescues. The lifeguards at Jones Beach are not ornamental. These are working lifeguards, professional lifesavers.

Roy Lester is a lifeguard's lifeguard. In his forty-plus years patrolling the waters of Jones Beach, Lester has rescued over one thousand people. He's won national lifeguarding competitions. He's even testified in court as an expert witness about lifeguarding. For Lester, nothing compares to the thrill of a rescue. "You're up there, and all of sudden you're going out in the water, and the rest of the world is behind you," he said.[2] "There's nothing else except between you getting from your stand to that victim. That's the only thing. And it's great. It's a great feeling."[3] Doubtful anyone has ever said that about a debtor's contingent claim.

At sixty-six, Lester is showing no signs of slowing down. These days he guards the calmer waters of a private beach club near his home. So why did he hang up his towel at Jones Beach? Because he wouldn't wear a Speedo.

In 2007, Roy Lester reported for his yearly swim test wearing a pair of jammers, a swimsuit that could pass for cycling shorts—formfitting but long, landing just above the knee. When he was on the job, he wore board shorts—a standard sort of swimsuit, long and loose-fitting. But swims tests are about speed. Regular swim trunks create drag in the water, and drag is the enemy of speed. Lester had tested in jammers for the past fifteen years. But that wasn't going to work this year.

Officials from the Office of Parks and Recreation, the organization in charge of the swim test, explained that participants can only take the test in an official Jones Beach Lifeguard swimsuit. Jammers were out. If he wanted to take the test, then he would have to wear trunks or a Speedo.

Lester was stuck. Trunks weren't an option, as they would slow him down. Nor was he willing to wear a Speedo. It was a matter of principle. Lester didn't feel comfortable wearing something as skimpy as a Speedo. Even though he is in incredible shape, and even though the swim test lasts less than two minutes, and even though he could have, in his words, "passed that test in dungarees,"[4] the Speedo wasn't going to happen. "Don't get me wrong," he said, "when I had a six-pack, I would wear a Speedo, too, but the six-pack days are a little beyond."[5]

Time being the operative measure. Roy Lester is not a young man. This is something he could not hide. He knew it, and so did his bosses, which is why he believes the Speedo was a means to get rid of older lifeguards like him. So Lester did what any lawyer-lifeguard would do: He filed a lawsuit.

The theory of the case was age discrimination. According to Lester, the Office of Parks and Recreation wanted to drive out older lifeguards, and the rule change was a way to make this happen. To support this claim, he cited internal documents from within the Office of Parks and Recreation, suggesting that older lifeguards might not be able to run across the beach during a rescue. For its part, the Office of Parks and Recreation rejected that age had anything to do with it. Weak swimmers were the intended target. Jammers are designed to boost a swimmer's speed. This wasn't about age, the Office of Parks and Recreation argued. It was about preventing weak swimmers from getting an unfair advantage.

The goal of a lawsuit is to get legal relief. For Lester, a win would mean damages—money to compensate him for his injury. But that's not what he really wanted. Roy Lester wanted to do his job. He wanted to take up his post at Jones Beach. He wanted to save lives. He didn't need damages. He needed an accommodation.

To accommodate is to adapt, to change circumstances and mold environments. To accommodate is to suspend the status quo. Accommodations are prosaic features of daily life. Consider how many times a day we accommodate others. Hold the door for someone whose hands are full. Clean up someone else's mess. Abandon the aisle seat so a family can sit together.

Accommodations are a powerful thing. When we make accommodations for others, we acknowledge our common humanity. As we rely on each other—as we give a little here, take a little there—we recognize the value of each other's lives. Even a brief accommodation is an exchange of information. And these exchanges become crucial experiences, as they force us to reckon with a harsh truth. The idea that all people are created equal is a legal command, not a practical description. We all have different needs and capabilities, different beliefs and wants. We accommodate not to erase these differences but to respect them. Accommodations are a vehicle to realize our ambitions, a functional means to make equality real for everyone in need of respect. Accommodations are a way to bring outsiders in.

Amanda Sapir knew what was coming.[6] It happened every time she went through a body scanner at the airport. She warned the Transportation Security Administration (TSA) officer that the scanner was going to flag her crotch. As she said that, a yellow square flashed onto the screen, just as it always did. It was her boxer briefs. The machine was confused.

The TSA officer asked Sapir how she would like to be identified. Sapir said she is gender nonconforming—female and also trans masculine. The officer had Sapir go through the machine again, but this time the officer entered Sapir's sex as male. The yellow square around her crotch vanished, only to be replaced by a new yellow square across her chest. It was her breasts. The machine was still confused. Sapir defied logic.

Next came the pat-down. The officer asked Sapir how she identified so the officer could conduct an appropriate search. "You get to decide how you are identified," the officer said.[7]

The pat-down proceeded and revealed the obvious—free of contraband, Sapir posed no threat to her upcoming flight. As she was leaving the security checkpoint, Sapir addressed the officer.

"Thank you," she said. "That was the kindest and most socially aware TSA experience I have ever had. Your thoughtfulness really means the world."[8]

This is accommodation at its finest. Sapir and the officer worked together, not as adversaries but as partners. Each was respectful of the other's predicament. Each gave the other space. And then there was the communication. Sapir and the officer talked the whole time. Sapir gave the officer a heads-up of what was about to happen. The officer responded with questions. When it became clear that the machine wasn't a viable option, they discussed terms of the pat-down. The exchange was pleasant and respectful. Choreographed to perfection, the exchange is a model for how security officers should interact with transgender people. Most importantly, it was easy. I'd be willing to bet that few of the passengers in line behind Sapir even noticed what was going on.

Which is, unfortunately, unusual for transgender passengers. Lindsey Deaton, a transgender woman, wrote an opinion piece called "Travel Can Be Traumatic for Transgender People," in which she describes her experience in secondary screening at Los Angeles International airport.[9] "I pulled my panties down and showed them I was carrying nothing. They turned away flinching and instructed me to stand still. One of the officers ran her hands up to the top of my legs, touching my tucked penis. I cried and shook through the whole experience," she said.[10] When she went to take a picture to document her experience, the officer in charge stopped her. "You can't take pictures, *sir*," he said.[11]

But nothing compares to the experience of Shadi Petosky, a transgender woman who live-tweeted her encounter with security in the Orlando airport.[12] In Florida to celebrate her birthday with her mother, Petosky was heading home to Minneapolis, where she runs an animation company. The body scanner turned up an "anomaly." It was her penis.[13] TSA officers directed Petosky to a private room, where they explained that she must go through the body scanner as a man. The officer also concluded that her hands failed the test for explosives residue, which meant that Petosky would require a full pat-down. Like in Lindsey Deaton's case, TSA officers said that Petosky could not take pictures of the encounter.

The encounter lasted forty minutes. In that time, Petosky underwent two full body pat-downs. TSA officers fully disassembled her luggage, in search of contraband that didn't exist. It was a crowded affair. All told, she interacted with two police officers, an explosives expert, and four TSA officers. And, of course, she missed her flight. But that wasn't even the worst of it. Afterward, Petosky was told that she would have to rebook and pay $955 for a new ticket. She reacted as anyone would in this situation—by turns offended and distraught. "They told me to get myself together," she tweeted. "I am sobbing, not belligerent."[14] Petosky finally made it out of Orlando that night, on a flight to Miami, not Minneapolis.[15]

The next day, a spokesman for TSA said that its officers acted in accordance with the organization's policy. "After examining closed-circuit TV video and other available information, TSA has determined that the evidence shows our officers followed TSA's strict guidelines," he said.[16]

Petosky responded by questioning the system that is in place. "I'm in trouble if they push a button that doesn't fit," she said. "Somebody saw me when I was getting into the machine and they decided to push a button."[17]

What explains the difference between Amanda Sapir's and Shadi Petosky's experiences with airport security? Why was one so easy and the other so hard? The answer is communication. The TSA officer talked to Amanda Sapir. She listened to what Sapir had to say. She took the time to understand her. Yet no one seemed to understand Shadi Petosky. She spoke up, but no one listened. And everyone lost because of it. The result was delay and hardship, inconvenience and hurt feelings. When communication breaks down, outsiders suffer.

Accommodations remake workplaces. Sometimes these changes are physical—think ramps and prayer rooms. More often than not, however, the changes are about personnel. Accommodation is a means for the law to make space for difference. It is a recognition that employees are not defined by their jobs, that they don't shed their identities when they come to work. Unlike the rest of civil rights law, which seeks to take identity out of the equation, accommodation law treats identity as its cornerstone. Accommodation is a call to action. Certain identities demand to be treated differently, and employers must take steps to facilitate that treatment. The failure to do so is itself a kind of discrimination.

The relationship between discrimination and accommodation is a knotty one. After all, accommodation looks a lot like discrimination. Say an employer schedules a devout Jewish employee to work on the Sabbath. The law may intervene on the employee's behalf. It may require the employer to shift the employee's schedule so as to avoid the conflict with the employee's religious practice. Although this may seem like discrimination in favor of the religious employee, we should resist thinking of it in this way. Accommodation is not a command to discriminate. It is not special rights. It is, instead, a means to combat inequality. Like a traditional case of discrimination—where the law strives to stamp out bias—accommodation seeks to make meaningful change in the way people access opportunities that would otherwise not be open to them. A safety net for difference, accommodation facilitates a way for outsiders to contribute without their identity getting in the way.

As a general matter, there are three characteristics of accommodation. The first is individuality. Accommodation breaks from the norm in civil rights law by treating claimants as individuals. Their identities are theirs alone. Disabilities are judged according to a particular claimant's needs and capabilities. Rather than a blanket category, disability is an umbrella category, capable of capturing a wide range of impairments. In the case of religion, there is no orthodoxy. Claimants can find their faith for themselves, and the law follows them on that journey. A Jew who keeps kosher but works on the Sabbath? Fine. A Catholic who is pro-choice? Sure. The law does not presume to define people's faith, but lets them figure it out for themselves.

The second characteristic of accommodation is negotiation. The law expects employers and employees to work these things out together, not as combatants but as collaborators. Conversation is crucial. Employees communicate what they need and why. Employers return with what, if anything, they can do to resolve the conflict. The conflict is what matters. Accommodation is a response to a conflict between the employer's needs and the employee's identity. Perhaps it's a scheduling issue, with the employer asking the employee to work on a religious holiday. Or it could be translation problem, if a deaf lawyer needs a translator to conduct a deposition. Whatever the identity, however it can be accommodated, the key is that employers and employees only become legal adversaries if they can't make it as partners first.

The third characteristic of accommodation is that it is limited. If it seems like the law bends over backwards to accommodate employees, actually the opposite is true. The law weighs heavily toward employers. Not only must accommodations be reasonable, but an employer's obligation ceases at undue hardship. Unfortunately, undue hardship isn't a self-explanatory standard, nor is its meaning consistent across civil rights law. In the case of religious discrimination under Title VII, an accommodation poses an undue hardship if it would cause more than a *de minimus* cost on the operation of the employer's business.[18] This is a relatively low standard for employers to resist accommodations. By contrast, disability law employs a more exacting standard. Under the Americans with Disabilities Act, undue hardship is means a "significant difficulty or expense."[19]

Accommodating difference is not the same as deferring to difference. The only way accommodation can work, as a legal mechanism, is if it its limits are real. Parties need to be able to anticipate how a dispute will be resolved. Claimants need to know when it makes sense to pursue a claim. Employers need to know when to resist a claim. And both sides need to know what a hard case looks like.

Roy Lester's lawsuit had a staccato feel to it, stopping and starting again on its way to trial. At one point, the case came to a complete standstill. The trial court rejected his claim outright, ruling that Lester did not raise an issue that needed to be resolved.[20] Trial courts exist to find facts, to determine what really happened in a given dispute. If there are no open facts, there's no need for a trial. The trial court effectively said that there was no fact in question. Lester appealed. In the summer of 2016, the appellate court revived Lester's case.[21] The appellate court ruled that the Office of Parks had not offered a legitimate reason why Lester could not opt to wear a more modest swimsuit.[22] In this context, legitimate means something specific. It comes from a prominent decision in which the Supreme Court outlined the necessary steps to proving an employment discrimination claim.[23] After the plaintiff makes a basic showing of discrimination, the employer gets to respond by showing that the employment action in question—here, the swimsuit requirement—was based on some nondiscriminatory reason. The appellate court concluded that the Office of Parks had not yet tendered such a reason.[24] This is not to say that it didn't have one, only that the Office of Parks hadn't volunteered it yet.

Onward to trial to sort it out. It's hard to say what will happen there. But there's something about the case that's worth considering, something that has been nagging at me since I first heard about the saga of the lawyer-lifeguard and the Speedo. If the Office of Parks was really trying to get rid of older lifeguards, would the Speedo really be their weapon of choice? Lester is not the only older lifeguard at Jones Beach, but he is the only one who refused to wear a Speedo for the recertification test. While there is a class of older lifeguards, Lester is in a subclass all by himself.

His case is textbook new discrimination. And like so many new discrimination cases, it is hard to pin down the exact wrong he suffered. Was it age, or the way Roy Lester in particular performed his age? Was it just modesty? Can you divorce modesty from age? In an interview with *This American Life*, Lester explained that he no longer felt comfortable in a Speedo, that he felt self-conscious about his body, and that people shouldn't have to feel self-conscious to do their jobs.[25] He was standing on principle. Sure, he could have just put the thing on for the test, which would have lasted all of a minute and twenty seconds. But it was the principle. The principle mattered to *him*. Ultimately, the case isn't really about older lifeguards. It's about Roy Lester.

In October 2011, Melissa Franchy boarded the B110 bus in Brooklyn, New York, settling into a seat at the front. After some time, a fellow passenger approached her, requesting that she move to the back of the bus. "This is a private Jewish bus," the man said, and women sit in the back. Franchy appealed to the driver for help, but his English was weak. From the back of the bus, a woman shouted, "Just move, I mean, that's the way it is. You don't ask."[26] The male passenger spoke up again: "When the Lord gives a rule, you don't question it."[27]

The B110 bus is a relic from another time—or perhaps place. The B110 connects Williamsburg and Borough Park, neighborhoods home to well-established Hasidic communities. Though it is part of the city's Metropolitan Transportation Authority (MTA) system, the B110 is not listed on MTA's Brooklyn bus schedule.[28] The buses themselves appear to be older than the rest of MTA's current fleet, and they often have signs in Hebrew on them. Plus, as Melissa Franchy learned that day, they're segregated by sex— men up front, women in the back.

Technically, the B110 is a franchise of the New York City Department of Transportation. Operated by the vaguely named Private Transportation Corporation, the B110 is the product of a public-private partnership, in which a private organization pays the government for the ability to run a public service. If the Private Transportation Corporation runs the B110 for the City, how can it segregate men and women?

It can't. Shortly after Franchy's story broke, Mayor Michael Bloomberg announced that such segregation ran afoul of New York civil rights law, and the Private Transportation Corporation posted signs to comply with the city's demands.[29] But the segregation continues, not by mandate but by custom.[30] As most of the B110 riders are Hasidic, they are free to segregate themselves, if they wish.[31]

The B110 is but one example of how ultra-Orthodox Jews try to balance their beliefs with life in a modern metropolis. For these Jews, accommodation is a fact of life. Their local post office is open on Sundays.[32] The local public pool has a female-only swimming period.[33] So as to satisfy ancient Jewish law about where their water comes from, Hasidic matzo factories installed special filters to qualify for a permit to draw from groundwater wells.[34]

As a legal mechanism, accommodation is a tool to solve conflicts. A perfect tool it is not. After all, accommodation is costly. Think of all the physical changes that must be made to accommodate people with physical disabilities—the ramps, the lifts, accessible bathrooms and workspaces, Braille translations, and much, much more. These are not imaginary costs; someone has to bear them. And think of the nonmonetary costs of accommodation. When an employer rearranges a schedule to accommodate an employee's needs, it is the employee's coworkers who bear the brunt of that change. The more accommodations we make, the more costs we incur.

My view is that accommodation is worth the cost. Equality demands it. That said, it does not apply in every case. Left unrestrained, accommodation would eventually swallow up civil rights law. Accommodation needs a limiting principle, and

I propose one in the final chapter. But for now let's stick to the particular accommodation at hand.

The B110 story shines a light on the central tension inherent in accommodation law. Who are we accommodating? I have told the seat saga from Melissa Franchy's perspective, but I could have also presented it from the standpoint of the Hasidic man. He holds a sincere religious belief about how men and women are supposed to interact in daily life. That some Jews—even some ultra-Orthodox Jews—reject his understanding is not the point.[35] This is a matter of faith for him, and his faith is worthy of respect. When Melissa Franchy got home from her trip, she likely complained to friends and family about the unreasonable man on the bus. The man likely said the same about the woman who threatened his faith. One woman's sex discrimination is another man's religious liberty.

In the world of accommodation law, easy answers are elusive. The law strives for balance. Take each case on its own terms. Consider the idiosyncrasies of the dilemma presented. Try to sculpt a fair result. What I like most about accommodation—and I will say this over and over again—is that it forces people to communicate. The conversation is what matters most. And that is, unfortunately, what was missing from Melissa Franchy's story. The real problem was not that men and women were sitting apart. No, the real problem is that Franchy did not have a chance to make her case. Conversation is the key.

Change is not linear. There is no batting average for progress, no win-loss records for equality. Much of the progress of civil rights happens outside the courthouse, in the spaces in-between lawsuits. For all the victories in court, there are many more in hallways and at dinner tables, on schoolyards and in parks. We should not think about civil rights in terms of wins and losses. Winning a lawsuit doesn't guarantee change. Nor does losing a lawsuit prevent change. Some losses still have wins in them.

Take Lakettra Bennett's case, for example.[36] Bennett took a job as a model at Abercrombie & Fitch ("model" is company speak for a sales position). She soon received a promotion to a manager-in-training position. The promotion came with a transfer to one of the company's Hollister stores. At the time, Bennett followed the company's "Look Policy," which required employees to wear clothing that was consistent with the Hollister brand: "ripped-up jeans, a little revealing, sporty, California beach style, laid back." Sexiness was key. The women of Hollister were expected to wear tight clothing that accentuated their bodies.

The dress code became a problem for Bennett after she converted to the Apostolic religion. Modesty became paramount for her. She exchanged her short skirts for long skirts that fell below the knee, her low cut shirts for long sleeve shirts that did not show any cleavage. On her first day at work following her conversion, she wore an ankle-length denim skirt, which was unlike anything Hollister had ever sold.[37]

Though her new appearance violated Hollister policy, the company wanted to work with her. Over the course of several meetings, the company offered several options to resolve the conflict between its dress code and Bennett's religious practice.[38] One option was to wear jeans instead of a skirt. Another was to wear a short skirt with leggings underneath to cover her legs. The final option was to look in other stores for skirts that would satisfy both the dress code and her religious beliefs.

Bennett rejected all three proposals. It was long skirts and nothing else. The only accommodation she would settle for was an exception to the company's dress code. But this Hollister would not do. So they gave her two weeks to make a decision: adhere to the policy or resign.[39] She opted to resign.[40] Soon afterward she sued the company, alleging religious discrimination under Title VII of the Civil Rights Act. She argued that the company failed to make reasonable accommodations for her religious practice.

Cut to the end. Bennett lost her claim, as she should have. Hollister did exactly what it was supposed to. The company heard her out. It considered the circumstances. And it gave her a range of options to deal with the problem. That she rejected them says more about her than it does about the company. The law promises *reasonable* accommodations. Bennett's request was unreasonable.

This is what happens when a company takes its accommodation obligation seriously. This is civil rights law working as it should. Civil rights law is a claimant-centric enterprise, but it should not defer to a claimant's every whim. This is often the hardest point to convey about accommodation. It is a slog, an uphill battle for claimants. Few will scale the summit.

If that's the loss, where's the win? Lakettra Bennett still made change. She defined her identity. She stood up for her faith. She communicated with her employer about who she is and how she wants to live her life. Her employer not only heard her, but worked hard to find a resolution. It may not look like much, but it is. It's easy to mark change when Congress passes groundbreaking legislation or when the Supreme Court hands down a consequential decision. Though important and influential, these are only moments in our lives. Change is as much about the small interaction as it is about the historic moment.

There is a longstanding divide in civil rights about the role of compromise in bringing about change. The divide pits those who push for wholesale change against those who favor an incremental path. Recall the fight over marriage equality. There were those who wanted to push for civil unions and domestic partnerships as a step toward full-blown marriage equality. Others took the view that equality meant marriage and nothing else.

The wholesale-incrementalism divide masks a vital lesson about social change. All change is incremental. Supreme Court decisions may change the law, but they do not change how everyone feels about the underlying legal issues. When Congress passed the Civil Rights Act in 1964, the law had its detractors, and it probably still does. Viewed through an historical lens, watershed moments occupy most of the picture. But that's the thing about a wide-angle lens: It doesn't capture the finer details of an image. Students will one day study the history and meaning of *Obergefell v. Hodges*[41] and the Obama administration's decision not to enforce the Defense of Marriage Act.[42] Yet they won't study the real agents of change. The gay family who moved in next door. The older gay couple whom you see regularly at services. The kid on your child's soccer team who has two moms. Your coworker who brings his partner to the company holiday party.

Lasting change is not legislated. It is not handed down by a court. Lasting change comes from within communities. And it happens gradually, one conversation at a time.

One of the great failings of modern civil rights law is its strict adherence to discriminatory forms. The law draws distinctions between different types of discrimination, establishing different rules and protocols for proving each type of claim. Roy Lester's case may look like an intentional age discrimination case, but it is really a failed accommodation case. This is true of many new discrimination cases. They arise not out of malice or overt bias, but because an employer is not willing to accommodate an outsider's identity.

For Lester, it was about his desire to wear a particular kind of swimsuit. Age clearly played a role in Lester's decision-making process: He did not feel comfortable, at his age, in the skimpier Speedo. Age drove *his* preference. This is not the same as saying the alleged discrimination was because of age. The wrong occurred when the Office of Parks chose not to honor Lester's preference.

Recall Darlene Jespersen, the bartender who did not feel comfortable wearing make-up. She went to court with an intentional sex discrimination theory. Yet hers, too, was really a failed accommodation case. She wanted an exception to the company's make-up policy. She didn't feel like herself when she wore make-up. She felt inauthentic, undignified. The make-up interfered with her ability to do her job well. The wrong in that case wasn't sex discrimination so much as the rejection of her personality. The casino didn't let Jespersen be Jespersen.

Rights should be tailored to wrongs. Civil rights law should respond to wrongs as they actually are. The most striking thing about Roy Lester's and Darlene Jespersen's cases—not to mention so many of the new discrimination cases discussed throughout the book—is how poorly they fit within existing doctrine. Roy Lester has to make his case about age in general rather than about his own discomfort with wearing a revealing swimsuit. Darlene Jespersen has to make her case about why make-up is gendered rather than about her own dislike of it. These are individuals making their cases about groups, and it doesn't really fit.

At an early stage of work on this project, I presented to the faculty of another law school for feedback. One participant thought I had Jespersen's case all wrong. He said the crux of her lawsuit was gender stereotypes. The problem with the casino's make-up rule, he argued, was that it burdened women by forcing them to conform to a stereotyped conception of femininity. Be pretty or you're out. There's something to this, no doubt, though I don't think that this was Darlene Jespersen's actual objection. Sure, she argued as such in her lawsuit because that's what the doctrine requires. But in her deposition, when she explained why she couldn't abide by the policy, she didn't talk about women. She spoke about how *she* felt about make-up, how it made her feel about her sense of self. At its most basic level, at the level of wrongs, the case was about Darlene Jespersen's personality.

The same is true of Roy Lester. Lester will go to trial, where he will argue that the Office of Parks was trying to squeeze out the older lifeguards. And maybe it was. But he may not have cared about that if the Office of Parks would have let him test in his jammers.

Floralba Fernandez Espinal worked at Unique Thrift, a second-hand store in the Bronx, New York.[43] For a retail position, the job was surprisingly physical. Espinal spent her shifts on her feet, lifting and carrying piles of clothing from the storeroom at the back of the store, to the showroom. This was her job, day in and day out, and she was fine with it. Until she became pregnant.

It's not uncommon for a pregnant woman to worry about her baby. Worry is perhaps the single emotion that unites all expecting parents. But Espinal had more reason to worry than most. Having miscarried the year before, Espinal was concerned, justifiably, that the physical stress of her job could endanger her child. So she talked to her boss. Could they temporarily move her to a different position? She could work the register, a job she had done before. Or she could tag or hang clothing. Other employees had done this before, substituting one task for another for a short time. Her boss told her to get a note from her doctor.

The note gave Espinal a sense of relief that had been missing in those first three months of her pregnancy. "No lifting, pushing or carrying heavy objects or loads," it said. Espinal carried the note in her lunch bag. The first thing she did once at work, even before clocking in, was give her boss the note.

But the note didn't generate the response she was expecting. Rather than discuss how they would deal with her physical limitations, her boss told her to get to work. Something wasn't right. Worry flooded back. Three hours later, Espinal's boss placed her on unpaid leave. The reason: She could no longer do her job.

Though shaken by the decision, Espinal kept her wits about her. She grabbed her cell phone and recorded a conversation with her boss. "But the only thing that they are saying in the letter is that I can't do heavy lifting," she said. The supervisor responded that employees have to be able to do everything at the store. Lifting, it turns out, was an essential part of the job. If she couldn't lift, she couldn't work at Unique Thrift. She could return to work, her boss said, when her restriction was over.

Floralba Fernandez Espinal was twenty-two years old, three months pregnant, and out of work. Born in the Dominican Republic, Espinal dreamed of going to college and becoming a teacher. But all that would have to wait. Right now she needed to focus on making rent and buying food.

Pregnancy poses a puzzle for civil rights law. Is pregnancy the same as sex, or is it a trait unto itself? The answer is critical, as it

determines the scope of the law. If they're the same, then pregnancy is a protected trait. If they're different, then pregnancy
falls beyond the reach of civil rights law. In 1976, the Supreme
Court said they were different, ruling that employers could single
out pregnancy without running afoul of Title VII of the Civil
Rights Act.[44] Two years later, Congress passed the Pregnancy
Discrimination Act of 1978 (PDA), which says pregnancy discrimination is a kind of sex discrimination.[45] The PDA is proof
that Congress listens when the Court speaks. Clearly it didn't like
what it heard.

The PDA is a curious statute. In addition to redefining pregnancy as sex discrimination, the PDA also contains a provision
that erects a barrier to accommodation. The provision says that
employers must treat pregnant women the same—no better, no
worse—than other employees who are subject to comparable
limitations. Because sameness is baked into the statute, pregnancy discrimination claims are all about comparisons.[46] Courts
are strict—no comparator, no claim.[47]

For Espinal, making a claim under the PDA would have been
an uphill battle. She would have needed to show that Unique
Thrift treated her differently than a male employee who likewise couldn't handle the physical aspects of the job. It's unclear
whether she could have proved this. I suspect she would have
been stuck. Luckily, she had another option.

In 2014, New York City adopted the Pregnant Workers
Fairness Act.[48] Like the PDA, the ordinance prohibits pregnancy
discrimination in employment. Unlike the PDA, however, the
ordinance mandates that employers make reasonable accommodation for pregnant employees. Espinal's union put her in touch
with lawyers from A Better Balance, a legal advocacy group in

New York City. The lawyers were able to do what the doctor's note couldn't.

Espinal got her job back.[49] The store agreed to give her a light duty assignment—hanging and pricing clothing, rather than hauling weighty piles of clothing. She kept her seniority with the company. And she received $1,088 in back pay.

This is what happens when accommodation is possible. No need for a comparator or an inquiry into how badly the company could have treated her. Just a question of whether it was reasonable for the company to keep her on staff during her pregnancy. It turns out it was. No drawn-out litigation and no hard feelings. Unique Thrift got to keep a dedicated employee, and Espinal got to keep her job when she needs it most. Importantly, the parties worked things out together. Civil rights law facilitated the conversation.

Can a college student bring a python to live in the dorm? The snake is an emotional support animal, not a pet, and the college will place the student in a single room. No roommate, just a student and a python.

This is, it turns out, a true story. A colleague mentioned this story to me, hoping to expose the folly of my project. Accommodate broadly, she used the example to say, and soon we'll all be living next door to a potentially large, potentially lethal snake.

Sometimes the silly examples make the strongest points. Once we start making accommodations, there is little to stop the slope from slipping. Now it's a python, but what comes next? A big cat. A wolf. An emotional support weapon. Even when there are limits in place, accommodation still feels limitless. To bend to the needs and preferences of one is to resist the needs and preferences of another. While the snake may be a critical resource for the student, it may be a major source of anxiety for another student. Let's not even consider what would happen if the snake escapes.

Extreme examples are a lawyer's stock in trade. If a rule can't hold, the rule isn't any good, so lawyers hunt for the example that frustrates the rule. Lawyers are forever looking for their dorm pythons.

I am the first to admit that accommodation is ripe for abuse. Some people will always take advantage of a legal subsidy, even if they don't really need it. But the point is that some do really need it. It's not really up to me to decide who is entitled to the law's protection. Nor am I a purist. I harbor a surprising amount of ill will toward the emotional support Chihuahua that a congregant regularly brings to my synagogue. I've made terrible assumptions about able-bodied people who park in handicap parking spots. And to the kid in my daughter's school with the peanut allergy, I apologize for everything I have ever said about you while struggling to spread sunflower butter on bread.

And yet I still believe in accommodation, and it's because of stories like this.[50] Years ago, IBM hired a Muslim woman who wore a veil. On her first day, she needed to have her photo taken for her ID badge. When she objected to the request to remove her veil, the company came up with a workable solution. She would get two badges. Her primary badge displayed a picture of her wearing the veil. As this was how she would look every day, it was how the security officers would recognize her. But the company also took a backup shot, one without the veil, in case they ever needed to identify her face. The company agreed that if the employee ever needed to show that badge, she would only have to do so to a female security officer.

A simple fix to a vexing problem.

What really happened that day at the swim test? Perhaps the brass at the Office of Parks and Recreation really were trying to get rid of the older lifeguards. Maybe this was all about Roy Lester, that he had become too bashful to do the job. It may have also been the result of a union dispute gone sour. Not only is there a lifeguard union, but Lester was the union's chief negotiator when the Speedo incident occurred. Maybe this was all just payback.

In his interview with *This American Life*, Roy Lester compared himself to Rosa Parks. When asked why he didn't just wear the Speedo for all twenty or so seconds of the test, he answered with a question. "Why didn't Rosa Parks just go to the back of the bus?" he said. "There were plenty of seats."[51]

It takes chutzpah to say that wearing a Speedo is anything like Jim Crow. I scoffed when I first heard it. But I've come to see it differently over time. Roy Lester is in the life-saving business. It's not what he does; it's who he is. And the Speedo is a harbinger of change. Roy Lester feels like his way of life is under attack. He feels like the Office of Parks and Recreation is trying to stop him from being himself. And I get it. This is why civil rights law exists. Not for old lifeguards who don't want to wear tiny swimsuits, but for people who feel like they are being excluded from civic life because of who they are. Roy Lester took a stand for lifeguarding as he's always known it. There's something to be said for that.

Equality Derby

Of all the events in the summer Olympics, there is nothing like the decathlon. Spanning two days, the decathlon brings together ten track and field events—four runs, three throws, and three jumps.[1] It is at once grueling and majestic, a true test of the limits of the human body. The winner is crowned the "world's greatest athlete," a moniker first given to American Jim Thorpe, in 1912, by King Gustav of Sweden.[2] To finish the event, even to come in last place, is a crowning achievement of a career in sport. As a sign of respect, all finishers, regardless of position, take a victory lap together.[3]

At the 1976 Olympic Games, in Montreal, Canada, American Bruce Jenner won gold in the decathlon.[4] Jenner's victory was decisive, setting a new world record. Though he may have competed by himself, Jenner carried a country on his back. Amid the backdrop of the Cold War, this was a win for the whole United States, a triumph of the American spirit. As the final event, the 1500-meter run, ended, a fan burst onto the track, carrying an American flag. The fan handed Jenner the flag, and Jenner ran with it. We've come to expect this scene as part of a gold medal moment, athletes celebrating with their country's flag in hand or draped over the shoulders. But this wasn't a tradition yet. Bruce Jenner was the first to do it.

Almost immediately, Jenner skyrocketed to fame in the United States. He became a spokesperson for Wheaties, starring in a popular commercial for the cereal brand. The commercial ran so often that *Saturday Night Live* based John Belushi's "Little Chocolate Donuts" skit on it. Jenner also cut commercials for Tropicana orange juice, Minolta cameras, and Buster Brown shoes. He graced the cover of magazines. He raced cars. He starred in movies, television shows, and music videos. Like other great athletes then and now, Jenner transcended his sport. He was a celebrity.

As it turns out, Bruce Jenner's celebrity was just a prelude to even wider fame. Years later, Jenner married Kris Kardashian, and together they built a media empire around their children. Multiple reality shows later, Jenner is probably more well-known today as the Kardashian sisters' stepfather than as a world-class athlete. But that may be changing.

In April 2015, Jenner sat with Dianne Sawyer for a special edition of ABC's *20/20*.[5] During their conversation, Jenner came out as transgender. "I'm me. I'm a person. This is who I am," Jenner said. "For all intents and purposes, I am a woman."

Three months later, Jenner appeared on the cover of *Vanity Fair* magazine, not as Bruce but as Caitlyn. Buzz Bissinger, a prominent sports journalist, wrote the cover story, while Annie Leibovitz, the celebrated portrait photographer, did the photo spread. This was unlike any coming out story ever seen.[6]

In the article, Jenner explains that this wasn't the first time she had undergone procedures toward transition. In the 1980s, Jenner took hormones and underwent electrolysis to remove her beard. She wore a bra and pantyhose underneath her clothing so she could feel authentic. But she was scared of how people would react, what it would mean for Jenner to stop being Bruce. Fame is a tricky thing: A piece of you belongs to the public.

Jenner's transition from Bruce to Caitlyn culminated in a visit to a plastic surgeon in Beverly Hills. As the *Vanity Fair* piece describes it, Bruce entered the office for facial-feminization surgery. Ten hours later, Caitlyn emerged. This is how Jenner draws the line. Any transition—be it gender or anything else—is a process. For Jenner, the facial-feminization surgery was the moment she started her new life.

"I Am Cait" premiered in 2015. A reality show in the same vein as its predecessor, "Keeping Up with the Kardashians," "I Am Cait" ran for two seasons on the E! network. Jenner served as an executive producer. The show picked up after Jenner's transition, documenting how she began her life as Caitlyn. Mostly, it focused on how Jenner navigated two kinds of relationships—her family and her celebrity. To the show's credit, it featured prominent members of the trans community along the way.[7] They served a dual function—guides for Jenner on her journey and ambassadors for the trans community at large. Though it hewed closely to the docudrama script, the show never shied away from its educational function. Caitlyn Jenner was never just a person. She was the embodiment of an identity, the public face of an outsider group.

Right around the same time Caitlyn Jenner introduced herself to the world, a similar story was simmering in Spokane, Washington. Rachel Dolezal, the head of the local chapter of the NAACP, had been outed—by her parents no less—as white.[8] Unlike Jenner, who relied on extensive surgery to realize her transition, Dolezal took a do it yourself approach. She used tanner to darken her skin.[9] She wore a weave in hair.[10] She married a black man.[11] She received a master's degree in fine arts from Howard University. She worked in furtherance of racial justice. She trained as a hairstylist specializing in black women's hair. She taught African American studies at a nearby university.

In an interview on NBC's TODAY show,[12] Matt Lauer asked Dolezal about her identity: "Are you an African American woman?" Her response was firm but not categorical: "I identify as black." She said she began identifying as black when she was as young as five, drawing self-portraits with the brown crayon. Lauer asked when she started "deceiving" people about her race, to which Dolezal responded by pointing to how newspapers described her in their coverage of her human rights work. A first story called her a "transracial" woman. The next story called her a "biracial" woman. And finally a story called her a "black" woman. She chose not to correct the record. When Lauer asked why, Dolezal said the issue is more complicated than true or false.

Dolezal's story unleashed a fierce debate about race and identity. Was she black or white? What does it actually mean to be black or white? Can people change their race? Was Rachel Dolezal transblack, or just a white woman in blackface?

Caitlyn Jenner and Rachel Dolezal. Two identities in motion. One became celebrated, the other loathed. One donned magazine covers and starred in her own television show, the other became a national joke. Why?

Civil rights is a contact sport. Outsider groups jockey for protection under the law. The stakes are high and the competition is fierce. With equality on the line, groups have to make the strongest case for themselves. Most do this by analogy. Outsider groups argue that they are like other groups who have come before them. They try to convince the decision-maker—be it court, legislature, or an individual person—that their struggle mirrors that of an earlier civil rights struggle. Protect us, they argue, because we are like them. Our rights are like their rights.

The comparison is usually to the black civil rights movement of the 1960s. This should come as no surprise. American civil rights law is closely tied to the history of African Americans in this country. Race discrimination is the cornerstone of civil rights; it is where the story begins. As each new chapter unfolds, it only make sense to link back to the beginning, to show that the current struggle is but a continuation of the struggles that came before it. Rather than a series of isolated events, civil rights is a cumulative project.

This mode of thinking is not without its critics. Some bristle at the comparison to the experience of African Americans. Not in this country, not with our nation's past. Analogies have rhetorical power, but they elide history. When new outsider groups take up the mantle of civil rights, what happens to the unfinished work of civil rights? How will we know when the law is stretched too thin? Because equality requires resources, and because resources are scarce, civil rights law pits groups against each other, in a kind of Equality Derby. Groups jockey for the law's protection. They push back against one another's claims. They make distinctions, all in the hope of securing their rights. This is a recipe not so much for disaster, but for the slow growth of justice.

This chapter is about history. It is about the path toward equality. It is about what, in the broadest sense, civil rights law is trying to accomplish. The organizing idea is that civil rights law has a complicated relationship to history. History is the reason civil rights law exists. The need to remedy the worst of what we, as a nation, have done and what those past acts have wrought for people today. If the past shapes the present, then civil rights law is an affirmative attempt to rewrite our future.

Yet civil rights law is not bound by history. Civil rights law prohibits race discrimination against white as well as blacks. It prohibits sex discrimination against men as well as women, religious discrimination against Christians as well as Muslims. A group need not have a deep history of oppression in order to enjoy the law's protection. Insiders are just as protected as outsiders. We do this because of history, but we don't look to history to do it.

I wonder if this tension is a feature of the system rather than a bug. Perhaps the law is driving at something grander in scope, a dynamic interaction between identity and equality. A vision that starts, but does not end, with yesterday's wrongs. It is a vision that seeks to balance the interests of the group and the individual, to negotiate competing expectations and remedy a diverse range of injuries. Threading this needle is no easy task, and civil rights law often falls short of its lofty goals. But the enterprise itself is worth taking seriously. The universe of wrongs is vast. Some wrongs feel ancient and constitutive, while others seem superficial by comparison. How do we reconcile this? How can we do equality work without relying exclusively on history?

Barnard College is a special place. From its perch on New York City's upper west side, Barnard has been educating young women since 1889. Like other women's colleges, Barnard was founded as a response to discrimination in higher education. At a time when women were excluded from university life, schools like Barnard created a dedicated space for women. Some schools have since opened their doors to men—like Sarah Lawrence and Vasser, which became coeducational in the 1960s. But not Barnard. Barnard remains committed to its founding mission of educating women.

But who counts as a woman? In the summer of 2015, right around the time Caitlyn Jenner first appeared on the cover of *Vanity Fair*, Barnard changed its admissions policy to admit trans women.[13] According to the new policy, Barnard will consider applicants who "consistently live and identify as women, regardless of the gender assigned to them at birth."[14] Later in the policy, in a Frequently Asked Questions section, the school further defines this standard. An applicant must "identify herself as a woman and her application materials must support this self-identification."[15] By this standard, sex is not a biological command but an experience. Students define their gender for themselves.

Nor does Barnard prevent students from transitioning during their time in school. Students who transition to male "remain eligible to earn a Barnard degree."[16] The policy is further confirmation that the concept of a women's college is changing. Indeed, Barnard is hardly alone in adjusting its rules to address the needs of transgender students. In 2013, Smith College rejected an applicant, who identified as female, because a financial aid form registered her as male.[17] "Smith is a women's college," her rejection letter said, "which means that undergraduate applicants to Smith must be female at the time of admission."[18] Smith has since changed its policy to admit transgender applicants, adopting a policy similar to Barnard's.[19] Wellesley College's policy diverges only to the extent that it welcomes applications from students who were born female but identify as neither male nor female.[20] Mount Holyoke likely goes the farthest of the prestigious women's colleges, drawing the line only when it comes to applicants who were born male and identify as male. Everyone else can matriculate.[21]

Not all women's colleges have opened their doors to transgender students, however. Hollins University, in Virginia, will only admit a student who was born male if the student has completed the "surgical" and "legal" process to transition from male to female. No longer eligible to receive a degree from the school, current students who transition from female to male must transfer to a different institution.[22]

Since their founding, women's colleges have been at the forefront of conversations about womanhood. Most of them began as a kind of finishing school for young women, a training ground for married life. Gradually, women's colleges shifted their focus, becoming the rigorous schools we know today. The question of how to treat transgender students seems like an existential challenge to the idea of a women's college. Some view transgender students as doing exactly what women's colleges teach their students to do—question norms, break down barriers, and rethink gender. Others wonder whether admitting transgender students—specifically, trans men—is a big step toward the end of female-only education. If the school admits trans men now, then it is only a matter of time until the school admits men who were born men.

Whichever side a person falls on, there is no question that the presence of trans men changes a women's college. It means men in classrooms and student leadership positions. It means men in dorms and bathrooms. It means making accommodations. Some accommodations may be slight, such as teachers remembering to ask students about their preferred pronoun. Others, like gender-neutral bathrooms and dorm assignments, are more complicated. But the biggest accommodation of all is just sharing space. Ultimately, the students are the one who must make the accommodations. They are the ones who will decide whether and how transgender students fit in on campus.

Barnard's mission statement is instructive. "As a college for women, Barnard embraces its responsibility to address issues of gender in all of their complexity and urgency, and to help students achieve the personal strength that will enable them to meet the challenges they will encounter throughout their lives."[23] College is a time of self-discovery, and not just about gender. For many students, college is their first opportunity to forge an identity all their own, a sense of self that is not determined by their family. Something important is happening on women's colleges across the country. As individual students are figuring out who they are, so too are their colleges.

Reality television and porn. These are the only jobs Rachel Dolezal has been offered since her story broke. In a 2017 interview in the *Guardian*, Dolezal explains the state of her life. Though she has changed her name, people recognize her wherever she goes. She applied for a position at the university where she used to teach, but her former colleagues pretended not to know her. She's on food stamps. She can't cover her rent. If it wasn't for a friend's help, she'd be homeless.[24]

Rachel Dolezal is a victim of our culture. In an age of public shaming, social media runs on outrage. Private lives become public sensations. As her search for identity became fodder for Twitter, Rachel Dolezal lost control of her own story. She stopped being an actual person. She disappeared.

Yet the anger about her endures. For many, Rachel Dolezal is a liar and a thief. She is appropriating black culture, reducing the black experience to a costume. Writing in the *New York Times*,[25] columnist Charles Blow said Dolezal's actions were "a spectacular exercise in hubris, narcissism and deflection." Blow rejects any comparison between Dolezal's identity and the real struggles of transgender people and transracial adoptees. Dolezal's actions, by contrast, were not motivated by a sincere attempt to claim an identity, but as means to cover up her deceit. "Dolezal's performance may have been born of affinity," Blow writes, "but it was based on a lie—one she has never sufficiently recanted—and her feeble attempts to use professorial language and faux-intellectual obfuscations only add insult to the cultural injury."[26]

There are, no doubt, troubling aspects of her story. One concerns her time in graduate school at Howard University, one of the nation's most cherished historically black universities. This was in 2002, and Dolezal—then Rachel Moore—was in a master of fine arts program at the school. She filed a lawsuit against the school and one of her professors.[27] The allegations concerned her financial aid award and a teaching assistant position that Dolezal didn't get. But there was another aspect of her case that really bothered her critics. Dolezal also claimed that the director of Howard's gallery removed her artwork from a student exhibition because of her race—that is, because she was white. Critics of Dolezal see this as the height of hypocrisy.

In the *Guardian* piece, Dolezal blames the race discrimination claim on her lawyer. "I didn't understand," she says. "I wasn't a law expert. I don't know precedents. I don't know all these strategies and ways to fight a case." The lawyer "latched on" to a comment by her professor, who suggested that her white relatives would pay Dolezal's tuition if she lost her scholarship.[28]

Another troubling aspect of Dolezal's situation concerns her work. When her story broke, Dolezal was the head of the NAACP office in Spokane. Although Dolezal had a history of human rights work, being black wasn't a requirement of the job. She could have done the work without presenting herself as black. Dolezal would likely respond that her job grew out of her identity and not the other way around.

The *Guardian* piece introduces some new information about Dolezal's upbringing, information that seems designed to excuse Dolezal's actions. Dolezal's parents were Christian fundamentalists, and they raised their children strictly. Dolezal was born at home, and her parents put "Jesus Christ" as the sole witness on her birth certificate. The family was poor. Dolezal wore homemade clothing and worked the family homestead. Her parents beat her and spoke in tongues. After her mother's health began to fail, the task of raising Dolezal's adopted brothers, all of whom were black, fell to a teenage Dolezal. She raised them like they were her own. Although she gravitated toward black identity as a small child—when she covered herself in mud and pretended to be kidnapped from Africa—her brothers were her conduit into black culture.

Had Rachel Dolezal not worked at the NAACP, would people have cared so much about her identity? Or imagine that she had a black ancestor, would her claims to black identity be more palatable then?[29] What's the real problem, the way she went about changing her race or that she tried to change her race in the first place?

Some identity shifts are based on ideology, like when a liberal becomes conservative, à la the comedian Dennis Miller after the September 11 attacks. Other identity shifts are grounded in spirituality, as when a person converts from one religion to another. And some shifts are based on biology, such as Caitlyn Jenner's. What drove Rachel Dolezal's shift?

Phoenix is a city of highways. In every direction, all across the city, concrete dissolves into vast horizon. The weather is harsh and the terrain harsher. Cars and cactus thrive. The sun is dogged, as is the traffic, and both get worse every year. The highway is the defining feature of modern life in Phoenix. A diverse population, rarely touching, following a common path. We share the space. We merge.

A few days after the 2016 presidential election, my wife was on a highway entrance ramp, preparing to merge. She was coming home after visiting an ill friend. The car behind her honked insistently. The light was still red. As the light turned green, the car abruptly switched lanes, pulling along the passenger side of her car. The driver, a middle-aged white man, started screaming at her. *Liberal. Dyke. Cunt. We won. Make America great again.* When she didn't respond, the man spit on her car and sped off. My wife was driving a tan Subaru Outback. My daughter's car seat was in the back seat. Her stroller was in the trunk. On the back of the car was a Hillary Clinton magnet.

Like an x-ray, the 2016 presidential election revealed deep fractures in our society. We are racked by anxiety. We're anxious about identity. We're anxious about the economy. We're anxious about geography. And so much more. The pressure points are intensifying. The distrust is palpable. The anger is worse. It is enough to make a man spit on a stranger's station wagon.

I started writing this book in the twilight of the Obama administration. At the time, it seemed like we were witnessing a singular moment in the arc of equality. Rights were on the march. President Obama made a concerted effort to broaden and strengthen the rights of outsiders. Same-sex marriage swept the land. Transgender students found refuge in public schools. Pay equality became a priority. Dreamers went to work. Identity had always been at the forefront of President Obama's public life, even before he entered politics. We will likely never see a president as comfortable as President Obama was sharing his search for identity. To the very end of his presidency, President Obama was a force of optimism. With hope as his ballast, President Obama firmly believed that equality is more than metaphor.

The 2016 presidential election, by contrast, did not instill confidence. The thrust of President Trump's campaign, from its *Make America Great Again* slogan to its harsh rhetoric about difference, was a rebuke of Obama's embrace of pluralism. It was a rejection of difference. If the road forward leads backward, then we can expect a rights recession.

For me, the scariest thing, aside from the anger, was the intense focus on language. Specifically, the way bias became wrapped in humor. President Trump railed against political correctness. When criticized for his own brash, and often insensitive, comments, he would explain that he was just joking. Liberals are too sensitive; they can't take a joke.

My wife spent part of her youth in rural Pennsylvania. She has long since moved away, but there are people there for whom she still cares a great deal. Yet the relationships are straining. When my wife posted a picture of our daughter playing at the public library with a boy with dark skin, one of her friends commented that someone should contact border control. My wife demurred, as did I and many others who saw it. Her friend said it was a joke. She accused my wife of turning her back on her roots, of losing her sense of humor. From the friend's vantage point, my wife was a traitor to her place.

The car spitter and border patrol commenter are engaged in a common project. They are pushing back against the march of rights. After all, the car spitter chose his words carefully—liberal, dyke, cunt—so as to reach beyond my wife, to denigrate whole classes of people. As for the border patrol commenter, I suspect she has limited experience dealing with immigrant populations. This wasn't about my daughter or the boy she was playing with. It wasn't even about immigrants. It was about how she felt about her own place in our society, about what her life is and is not. Somehow this young boy became a mirror.

For all the talk of the world getting flatter, of technology bridging gaps and hastening communication, we seem to be drifting apart. As we move in different directions, the ties that bind us, as Americans, grow weaker. Our inability to communicate is concerning. We spit when we should talk. We mock when we should engage. It's getting harder and harder to merge.

There is no one civil rights law. Civil rights law is not a thing; it is a collection of things. An umbrella term that covers a wide range of legal regimes, civil rights touches many aspects of life. Whether it is police brutality or voting rights, employment discrimination or school desegregation, the charge of civil rights law is to right wrongs. No matter the domain, the common denominator is always equality.

In some areas of civil rights law, history takes center stage. Take equal protection law, for example. Although the text of the Fourteenth Amendment makes no mention of history or discrimination, the courts have made history a critical part of the equation. Not all forms of governmental action receive the same kind of scrutiny under the Equal Protection Clause. Some kinds of governmental actions—most notably, those that draw racial classifications—are deemed to be especially dubious.[30] Rather than a presumption of constitutionality, these actions receive more searching review by the courts.[31] Put another way, the government has to have a pretty good reason for passing such a law.

The genesis of this framework, amazingly enough, is a footnote in a 1938 Supreme Court case.[32] There, the Court noted that bias can influence the political process, specifically bias against "discrete and insular minorities."[33] Concerned that the usual mechanisms that protect minorities may not be able to withstand the forces of prejudice, the Court suggested that such laws might require extra careful review by the courts. Since then, the courts have run with the idea, developing a rich jurisprudence of suspect classes. One of the factors courts must consider, in deciding whether to intensify their review, is if the group in question has faced a history of unequal treatment.[34]

The Supreme Court has never said how much discrimination is enough to meet this standard. Nor has it laid out a formula for how long a group must face discrimination before it becomes entitled to protection.[35] Rather than speak in absolutes on the subject, the Court tends to reason by analogy, looking to deprivations that have already triggered heightened review. The default comparison, not surprisingly, is the experience of African Americans. From a civil rights perspective, slavery and Jim Crow are the apex of wrongs, the catalyst for all of equality law.

Understandably, they have become the benchmark against which all future wrongs are judged.

Few groups can come anywhere close to this standard. In the Equality Derby, the deck is stacked against any group who wants to broaden the reach of equality law. Some may argue that this is as it should be, that discrimination against African Americans belongs in a class all by itself. For what it's worth, I agree with this sentiment. A recent study found that black people are far more likely than whites to be wrongfully convicted of murder, and that innocent blacks had to wait longer than their white counterparts to be exonerated.[36] Racial bias oozes out of every part of this story, from arrest to conviction to freedom. Equality is a work in progress. We still have much to do in our search for racial equality.

Other parts of civil rights law don't incorporate history into the conversation. Under Title VII of the Civil Rights Act, for example, history is not part of the principal doctrine.[37] Unlike the Equal Protection Clause, Title VII takes a neutral posture toward identity. There are no levels of scrutiny, no forms of heightened review. All protected traits stand on level ground.

That is not to say that history didn't play a role in crafting the framework. It surely did. Congress passed the Civil Rights Act in response to racial segregation in civic life. The purpose of the law was to excavate norms that were buried deep in our culture. The Civil Rights Act looked at once forward and back. The law set out to make a break from the past, to create the American ideal anew.

Though it is grounded in history, the Civil Rights Act does not depend on history to function. Instead, it takes aim at classifications.[38] There are areas where the Civil Rights Act focuses on group discrimination—such as disparate impact claims or systemic discriminations cases. But the heart of the statute lies in individual experiences of discrimination. This is why I have always bristled when the civil rights doctrine speaks of protected classes. To prove a case of intentional discrimination under Title VII, a claimant must show that the claimant belongs to a "protected class."[39] This makes it seem as if the statute protects designated groups against discrimination. It does no such thing. Perfectly clear on its face, the law targets employment actions because of an *individual's* race, color, religion, sex, or national origin.[40] The statute doesn't refer to protected groups or classes. It does not address the subordination of racial minorities or religious minorities or women. The individual is its focus.

It is understandable why the law gravitates toward the group as its organizing unit. Every time someone is fired because her race, it adds another thread to a growing tapestry. Viewed through the lens of the group, the work of civil rights is to upend history, to reset a course. When the group is the focal point of the analysis, history is everything. The larger the tapestry, the harder it becomes to turn our backs. The larger the tapestry, the harder it becomes to care about the bald woman, or the smelly colleague, or the woman's whose faith compels her to end conversations with a prayer. Without a history of subordination, outsiders tend to fade away.

Please don't get me wrong. Being part of a group is a precious thing. Group members share a common history. They speak a common language. To be part of a group is to walk in the footsteps of those who came before you. The promise of group membership is a community based on shared experience. It makes no difference where you are or where you've been. You may be the only person for miles who has your identity. Yet you can always connect with others like you. This is what makes Dan Savage's *It Gets Better Project* so powerful.[41] Savage, an influential sex-advice columnist, sought to create a vehicle to reach gay youth who are victims of bullying. The immediate goal of the project was to urge gay kids not to commit suicide in the face of harassment and social ostracism. The broader aim, however, was to show these kids, many of whom have no gay role models in their day-to-day lives, that they belong somewhere, that there are people just like them. It tells kids that they're loved no matter what.[42]

Groups matter. I would never suggest otherwise. My hope is to find a way for civil rights law to acknowledge history without sacrificing other equality ventures. My concern is that civil rights law has lost sight of the individual at a time when individuality is more important than ever. Though it may seem inevitable, the Equality Derby is not essential. There is a way to strike at the full spectrum of discrimination as it exists today. Civil rights law should care about the individual. Not as much as it cares about groups, maybe much less so. But the universe of identities is vast. Civil rights law can do a better job of broadening its reach. Outsiders matter, too.

The statistics are discouraging. Transgender people are four times more likely to live in poverty.[43] They have significantly higher rates of suicide attempts than the general public (41%, compared to 4.6%).[44] And they face staggering levels of physical and sexual violence.[45] For most transgender people in the United State, life isn't easy.

Caitlyn Jenner is not like most transgender people. She lives in a three-bedroom house atop mountain in Malibu, overlooking Catalina Island.[46] She appears regularly in advertisements and other media. And she is recognized wherever she goes. In an age of celebrity obsession, Caitlyn Jenner is one of our culture's most famous faces.

There are downsides to fame, of course. Jenner had to transition in public, under the watchful eye of the paparazzi who follow her every move. She went through an experience that is fraught under ideal circumstances, and she had to do it in public. It couldn't have been easy.

Rachel Dolezal, by contrast, transitioned in private. She didn't seek the spotlight. She didn't invite television cameras into her home. She didn't seek public commentary on her life choices. She never asked to be the face of anything, and yet her shaming was very public. Had she lived in an earlier time, before Twitter and Facebook and clickbait stories absorbed our attention, Dolezal would have become, at worst, a local oddity. And that's only if her story ever leaked out. Had it not, she could have remained a pillar of the black community in Spokane.

Groups act as their own gatekeepers. They decide who makes the cut. The overwhelming chorus seems to be that Rachel Dolezal isn't part of the group. She's a charlatan, an outsider pretending to be an insider. If authenticity is the standard, Rachel Dolezal is a counterfeit black person.

This is a tricky thing, however, because groups aren't monolithic. Though they may be based on shared experiences, groups are made up of individuals, and individuals don't always agree. In an interview in *Vanity Fair*, pop star Rhianna called Dolezal a hero.[47] "Is it such a horrible thing that she pretended to be black?" she said. "Black is a great thing, and I think she legit changed people's perspective a bit and woke people up."[48] This is, of course, a qualified endorsement, if she *pretended* to be black. But it's an endorsement nonetheless. Interviewed on MSNBC, sociologist Michael Eric Dyson suggested Dolezal might be black in a cultural sense.[49] "She's taken on the ideas, the identities, the struggles," he said. Dyson undercut his praise, or at the very least, courted controversy with his very next sentence: "I'd bet a lot more black people would support Rachel Dolezal than, let's say, Clarence Thomas."[50] A nice example of how easy it is for fractures within a group to develop.

One of the strongest defenses of Dolezal came from law professor Camille Gear Rich, in an opinion piece on CNN's website.[51] According to Rich, "I will not indict her for her choice to link herself to this community, and I would consider her claim no greater if she identified a long lost African ancestor."[52] For Rich, choice is paramount. "We should not have to be slaves to the biological definition of identity, and we should not use race or gender identities as weapons to punish one another."[53]

But here's the real question: Why do any of us care, and why do so many of us care so much? On the scale of racial oppression, Rachel Dolezal's identity is small potatoes. In a piece in the *Atlantic*, Ta-Nehisi Coates argues that Dolezal's story is a distraction.[54] Kalief Browder's story, Coates argues, is what people should be talking about. A teenager from the Bronx, Browder was arrested for allegedly stealing a man's backpack. Browder proclaimed his innocence. Although it wasn't Browder's first brush with the law, the case should have been quick. Prosecutors had little to go on, and the victim proved unreliable. It was anything but quick, however. Browder spent three years imprisoned on Rikers Island, the bulk of it spent in solitary confinement. He never went to trial.[55]

Kalief Browder got lost in the criminal justice system. He fell through the cracks, and it ruined his life. He left prison after prosecutors dropped the charges against him. But he struggled on the outside. The scars of solitary confinement were too deep. Less than a month after his twenty-second birthday, Kalief Browder committed suicide.

"It is the oppression that matters," Coates writes. The media's fascination with Rachel Dolezal would "wither and blow away" if it wasn't for the oppression. People masquerade as things they're not all the time, Coates reminds us. But the attention paid to Dolezal is exceptional. "What fuels the fascination is the way it taps into one of America's greatest and most essential crimes— the centuries of plunder which birthed the hierarchy which we now euphemistically call 'race,' " Coates writes.[56]

The world is wrong. You can't put the past behind you. It's buried in you; it's turned your flesh into its own cupboard. Not every- thing remembered is useful but it all comes from the world to be stored in you.[57]

Claudia Rankine's *Citizen: An American Lyric* is a force of na- ture. It is the kind of art that plants itself inside you, anchored just beneath your nerves, capable of stinging you long after reading it. An amalgamation of poetry, essay, and visual art, *Citizen* offers a critique of racial bias in present day America. The sideway glances from strangers. The hurtful comments from dear friends. The man who leaves his briefcase open on the passenger seat of his car because he knows he'll be pulled over by the police. The demonization of tennis superstar Serena Williams because her body is stronger and blacker than the tennis world can handle. The abandoned people in an arena after a devastating Hurricane. The violence, the sheer terror and routineness of it. The stories in *Citizen* are like a punch in the chest.

Reading *Citizen* is a stark reminder that law is not medicine. Lawyers do not have the tools to alleviate pain. This is especially true of pain that is inherited, passed down from one generation to another, the kind of pain that is baked into people's DNA. We are at our most fragile when we're out in the world, exposed to the elements, confronted with the indignities of everyday life. Law is a means for resolving conflicts but not healing wounds. Law compensates and punishes, but it does not erase. A legal remedy is not an actual remedy. Law doesn't cure.

In an interview in the *Paris Review*, Rankine discusses a critical element of her work, the distinction between her personal self and her historical self.[58] She tells the interviewer, "I was always myself and a black person in the United States."[59] This idea is reflected directly in *Citizen: sometimes your historical selves, her white self and your black self, or your white self and her black self, arrive with the full force of your American positioning.*[60] We cannot shed our identity's past. The pain compounds over time. *Yes, and the body has memory.*[61] This is why the little things hurt so badly. This is why the little things aren't so little.

Years ago I was on a flight from Chicago to Los Angeles, fresh from a visit to see family. At the time, I was reading a lot about race discrimination, trying to fill in gaps in my legal training. That day I was about a third of the way through Randall Kennedy's book *Nigger: The Strange Career of a Troublesome Word.*[62] Once in my seat at the back of the plane, I pulled out Kennedy's book and dug back in. Engrossed in my reading, I didn't realize the girl was standing over me. A family of three had come to take their seats. The parents were to sit in the middle and aisle seat across from me. Their daughter, maybe fourteen or fifteen, was assigned to sit next to me. But the girl wasn't taking her seat. She was frozen, aghast, staring at me. It took me way too long to figure out why.

When I realized what was going on, rather than put the book down or tell her what the book was about, or engage her in any way whatsoever, I rotated in my seat, turning the book toward her. I wanted her to see that it was legitimate scholarship. I couldn't remember if Kennedy's picture was on the back cover. Hopefully she would see that the author, like her, was black. Hopefully she would see that I meant well, that her aisle seat was a safe space. She sat down. It took a few beats before she started crying. Her parents were quick to console her. As they huddled, looking over at me, I quickly stashed the book in my bag, trading it for the only other book I had with me—a collected volume of essays on black men, gender, and sexuality. Not the fix I was looking for. I apologized, lamely. She didn't change seats, though she never even looked at me during the flight. I read the in-flight magazine and pretended to sleep. I didn't get up to use the bathroom.

Say what you will about uncomfortable moments, but this wasn't the time for one. Of course I was free to read whatever I want. But that wasn't the issue. I didn't regard this girl. Though she was young, she understood enough of the world. She was aware of her historical self, and mine as well. Her body remembered.

There is discrimination and then there is Discrimination. The American civil rights tradition marked a turn away from one of the ugliest aspects of our country's history—bondage, redlining, poll taxes, segregated existences. Civil rights law is our attempt to make good on the law's promise of equality. To do this, we have to look forward and back. Some wrongs are buried so deep in our bodies that we can't stop trying to treat them. Yes, we need a new civil rights. But the new must stem from the old. In the coming chapter, I propose a new doctrinal framework for civil rights. This framework seeks a delicate balance, to regard history without being constrained by it. There is still much work to do.

It was inevitable that people would make the comparison between Rachel Dolezal and Caitlyn Jenner. Both are engaged in a public campaign about identity and tolerance. Both have become representatives of their causes. Jenner is the face of a movement that has gained significant ground—legally, politically, and culturally—in recent years. Dolezal occupies a murkier space, but that has not stopped her from advocating for her right to define who she is. Whereas Jenner stands on the shoulder of countless trans pioneers, Dolezal is charting a new course. Perhaps she will be remembered differently by history.

Whatever their differences, the most important similarity between the two of them is that they're talking. Equality requires communication. Civil rights is about standing up for yourself and others, about defending a principle. For Jenner and Dolezal, that principle is self-definition.

In an interview in 2015, Dolezal compared her own search for identity to Caitlyn Jenner's.[63] Although she doesn't think of herself as a black person born in a white person's body, and she rejects the term "transracial" to describe herself, she still sees a parallel with Jenner. "Caitlyn Jenner has not been seen as a woman, and treated as a woman by other people, for her entire life," she said.

But this isn't about her or Jenner. It's about everybody. "I hope we can reach some kind of term for the plurality of people and allow everybody to be exactly who they are on the spectrum of all these things. Religion, gender, race."

I wonder what Caitlyn Jenner would say about that.

PART THREE

The Future

Accommodating Difference

On the wall of my office is a framed print. Surrounded by a smattering of smaller pieces, the print stands out in the crowd. A shock of bright red, with bold white letters and a thin white border, the print shows three dolphins leaping out of the water. The phrase "utopia in our time!" appears underneath them.[1] Sure, it's a little cheesy, but the print is meaningful for me. Frankly, I need the reminder. Equality is worth fighting for. I want my students to see it, too. We don't talk a lot about justice in law school, but we should. Lawyers are uniquely positioned to do good in the world. And a little magical thinking goes a long way.

When I first started working on this book, I described it to a colleague as utopian. She bristled at the word. Although I meant it in a good way, she thought I was being self-deprecating at best, and self-destructive at worst. Time is a prominent feature of academic life. Freedom is not just a perk but a precondition. Academics are supposed to discuss and engage, debate and critique. We are supposed to think things through to the end. And so my colleague and I went down the rabbit hole. She thought that utopian cannot have a positive connotation. I believe it can be a virtue.

Legal scholarship occupies an awkward place in the world of ideas. Law is a practical medium. Its data points are real cases—real cases involving real people who have very real problems. Reality is like a gravitational force, tethering legal theory to the ground. Legal scholarship exists in a pitched battle between aspiration and actuality. The best legal scholarship, the stuff that really moves me, is work that bridges theory and practice, scholarship that brings the world to bear on matters of doctrine. Good scholarship can be as stirring as good art. Good scholarship can stimulate the senses. Good scholarship can engender a universe of feelings, ranging from outrage to relief to hope.

What follows is a proposal for the next phase of civil rights law. The proposal is built atop three pillars. The first is that difference is universal. Normality is an allusion. Difference is a defining part of the human experience. The one thing we all share in common, despite our race or sex or religion or whatever, is that we don't fit in in some way. The second pillar is that these differences matter. Difference defines us. The things that set us apart from one another, the things that make us stand out—these attributes shape the way we experience the world. So much of civil rights law is about peeling away difference, about convincing ourselves that identity doesn't (or shouldn't) matter. What if civil rights law was organized around the experience of being an outsider? What if the law nurtured difference? How might that change the way people make their way in the world?

The third pillar is that conversation is a pathway to change. My proposal is designed to inspire contact. Let people talk about their needs and expectations. Make them give reasons for their decisions. In matters of identity and equality, information is crucial. If I could boil down my critique of existing civil rights law to a single point, it would be that the law doesn't encourage interaction. My argument is that conversation can go a long way to stop discrimination before it happens. If we can get people talking, then maybe they'll give reasons. If we can get people to give reasons, then maybe they'll find common ground. If we can get people to find common ground, then maybe we won't need civil rights law anymore. Maybe then change will start to happen on its own.

Susan Faludi's father was a shapeshifter.[2] Born to a well-off Jewish family in Hungary, he began life as Istvan Friedman. He survived the Holocaust by passing as a gentile. Convincing in this role, he was able to save his parents by posing as an officer in the Arrow Cross Party—a far-right political party that controlled Hungary at the time. After the war, he changed his name to Istvan Faludi. He left Europe for Brazil, then made his way to America, where he became Steven Faludi. In America, Steven found work as a photographer and a film retoucher. He started a family, moved to the suburbs, and took up extreme sports, like ice climbing, distance cycling, and rock climbing. A stern man with an abusive streak, Steven did not find peace in the home. After he and his wife separated, Steven returned to their home, in violation of a restraining order, to attack his ex-wife's new boyfriend with a baseball bat and knife.

Susan Faludi and her father were not close. After he moved back to Hungary, the two didn't speak much. Susan went on to great success as a writer. She won a Pulitzer Prize for a piece in the *Wall Street Journal* about the human costs—the lost jobs and, worse, lost lives—of the leveraged buyout of the Safeway chain of grocery stores.[3] She's written books about the September 11 attacks,[4] the backlash against feminist activists,[5] and the state of masculinity in American culture.[6] Feminism plays an important role in her work, and she credits her father's raw aggression for framing how she sees the world.[7]

In 2004, with a forged doctor's note in hand, Steven Faludi traveled from Hungary to Thailand, where he underwent sex reassignment surgery. Steven Faludi's masculinity was rivaled only by Stefánie Faludi's femininity (she had a collection of Marilyn Monroe outfits). After transitioning, Stefánie Faludi embraced life in a way she never had before. She made contact with Susan, hoping to reestablish a relationship. That email, and the resulting visits that flowed from it, led to Faludi's recent book, *In the Darkroom*.[8] Unlike her previous works, *In the Darkroom* is a memoir, in which Susan Faludi turns her critical eye inward, examining what her father's shape-shifting has wrought in her own life. The result is a meditation on identity in the modern world, and it's telling where Faludi ultimately lands.

Appreciating her father's life as a series of opposing forms—man/woman, American/Hungarian, Jew/Christian—Faludi takes a broad view of identity, capturing the full sweep of her father's life.[9] Fittingly, *In the Darkroom* ends with Stefánie Faludi's death. Faludi goes to the hospital, where she meets the doctor who cared for Stefánie in her final moments. The doctor can't give a precise cause of death, offering a smattering of possible ailments: "Sepsis, heart problem, stroke. Could be anything."[10] The doctor took Faludi to see the body, which was housed on the female wing of the hospital. There, starring at her father's body, Faludi decided that the only real divide in the universe is between life and death.

"Either you are living or you are not," she writes. "Everything else is molten, malleable."[11]

I find myself drawn to this idea. Identity is a lifetime process, on ongoing and ever-evolving narrative of our lives as we are experience them. The standard narrative of Stefánie Faludi's life might be that her struggle with identity was a prelude to her final transition in life. Stefánie was always buried beneath the surface. Istvan Friedman, Istvan Faludi, and Steven Faludi were just layers waiting to be peeled away. Becoming Stefánie was an excavation, an unearthing of her true self. I think we should resist this way of thinking. The shifts along the way are not stepping stones to some master identity. They are not artifice or folly. Shifts are a part of being human. The meaning of a person's race may change over time. Masculinity and femininity ebb and flow. I can speak with great precision about how my Jewish identity has evolved, and devolved, over the course of my life. Messiness is the natural order of identity. We live our lives in context. Which is why I think identity is not the best organizing unit for civil rights law. Personality makes more sense.

The first step is to define the nature of the right. From a structural perspective, the right to personality borrows from the religious discrimination under Title VII of the Civil Rights Act. In that domain, employees have wide latitude to determine the character and extent of their religion. The statute does not determine what counts as religion, nor does it mandate a particular strand of faith. Employees who align themselves with a mainstream religion are not expected to fall in line with the strictures of their faith. A lapsed Catholic and a devout Catholic stand on equal footing. The Jew who keeps kosher is no more Jewish than the Jew who eats cheeseburgers. The absence of faith doesn't even disqualify an employee from being protected against religious discrimination.

I am particularly interested in the way civil rights law bends the notion of religiousness. Rather than determine what is and is not religious, the law leaves that to the employee. The hallmark of religious discrimination law is that the law gives employees' space to define faith for themselves.

There are limits, however. The law cabins religion in two distinct ways. First, to count as religious for purposes of religious discrimination law, the belief or practice must occupy a place in the employee's life that is normally held for religion.[12] Put another way, the belief or practice must be like a religion in the employee's worldview. This explains how religious discrimination law sweeps beyond traditional religion to capture, for instance, moral and ethical beliefs. Take vegetarianism. The law does not distinguish between vegetarianism that is rooted in religion, as in the case of Hinduism, and vegetarianism that is based solely on the ethical treatment of animals. Both can be religious for purposes of employment discrimination law.

Vegetarianism is perhaps too easy an example. White supremacy offers a much tougher case. A case out of Wisconsin involved an employee who was a reverend in the World Church of the Creator.[13] His employer learned of the employee's racial views after a local newspaper featured him in a story about the church. By letter, the employer demoted the employee, citing the employee's involvement in the church as the reason for the demotion. From the employer's perspective, this was a sound personnel decision, a reasonable response to objectionable behavior. The employee thought it was discriminatory. And so did the court. A belief system need not have a concept of God to be religious, the court concluded.[14] What matters more is that the employee holds the belief with the same strength as one would hold a religious conviction.[15]

The second limit on religion comes in the form of a sincerity test.[16] Courts inquire whether the employee's belief is sincerely held. The purpose of this test is to weed out sham claims of faith. Because religion is a protected trait, and because courts give employees wide latitude to find their faith, there is an incentive to use religion to escape or modify work. Don't want to work a specific shift, claim a religious objection. Think you shouldn't have to cover your tattoos, say they are part of your religious practice. The sincerity requirement is meant to bring legitimacy to the process.

For example, a case in New York turned on whether a Muslim man's facial hair was part of his religious practice.[17] The man worked as a waiter at various hotels throughout New York City. When he booked a job at the Waldorf Hotel, the hotel provided him with a copy of their appearance code, which included a restriction on facial hair. When the man appeared for the event, he had just shy of a week's worth of facial hair on his face. Waldorf staff would not let him work, citing the violation of the appearance code. The man said the facial hair was religious in nature. But this didn't make a lot sense. The man never told anyone at the Waldorf about his religion before, and he had worked there for fourteen years. The man didn't say he recently converted to Islam or that he had become more devout, either of which could have explained his sudden change in appearance. He simply couldn't explain why, after many years of being clean-shaven, his faith now required him to have a beard. Nor did it help his cause that he completely shaved off the facial hair three months after the incident and continued to work at the Waldorf. Ultimately, the court concluded that this was not a genuine claim of faith.[18]

Is religion special?[19] I believe it is, and not because of its connection to faith or because the role central role religion played in the founding of America. Religion is special because it is boundless. Sometimes it is indeed a matter of faith. Other times it is about a guiding moral code. And sometimes it is just a metaphor for describing how important something is to us—the things we do *religiously*. Religion is a lens into what people care about most.

In her best-selling memoir *Wild*, Cheryl Strayed writes about her mother's devotion to horses. "Horses were my mother's religion," she said. "It was them she'd wanted to be on all those Sundays as a child, when she'd been made to put on dresses to go to mass."[20] She doesn't mean that her mother actually thought horses were divine. She's talking about the role that horses played in her mother's life, how they were central to her mother's being.

This book is filled with stories about people who define themselves around aspects of their identity that they hold dear. Be it horses or vegetarianism, an aversion to make-up or a passion for lifeguarding, the thing itself isn't what matters. It's the person's relationship to the thing. That's what the law should protect.

My vision of the right to personality is that it should protect aspects of our identity that cut to core of who we are. The scope of the right won't be determined by a preexisting list of traits, but by individuals themselves. Up to now, the work of civil rights law has been to stamp out certain kinds of bias. The future of civil rights should be about letting people be themselves.

For instance, consider Deborah Marks.[21] Marks worked as a telemarketer, but she wanted more from her sales career. In her first year at the company, Marks won the "Telemarketer

of the Year" award. The following year, she was denied a promotion to a face-to-face sales position. Her appearance was
the sticking point. They wanted someone prettier, someone
thinner. In an outside sales setting, her supervisor said,
presentation is everything. "Lose the weight and you'll get
promoted," he said.[22]

Marks protested, but the supervisor would not budge, and the
matter ended up in court. Like many outsiders, Marks's claim
defied easy categorization. Was it weight discrimination? Was it
beauty bias, or perhaps some combination of the two? No, Marks
built her case around sex, as neither weight nor appearance is a
protected trait under the Civil Rights Act. There is a natural argument to make here. Conceptions of beauty are steeped in gender
stereotypes. Fat is not pretty. Fat is not feminine. Men can be fat.
Women cannot.

Marks made a sex discrimination argument not because it felt
right, and not because it explained what actually happened, but
because that is where the doctrine pushed her. That was the only
pathway available, and it led nowhere. This was weight discrimination, the court ruled, not sex discrimination. Marks could not
prove otherwise. Being a great salesperson was not enough. The
look mattered more.

Everyone gives up something when they go to work. This
comes with the territory of participating in civic life. But the
question is: When do we give up too much of ourselves? When
do we stop being who we are?

My suggestion is that personality discrimination should track
discrimination against religion. The point is not that personality
is religion, but that the law should do with personality what it
does with religion. Specifically, the question of what counts as
personality will fall to the individual. Courts will adopt a neutral

posture, deferring to a person's vision of her own life. The right is not boundless, however. The same limits that apply to religion would apply here: The personality has to occupy a central place in the person's life, and it must be sincere. Centrality will be harder to prove than sincerity. Sincerity is a matter of frequency and commitment. Centrality is more elusive. More than a mere preference, centrality speaks to deeply held convictions, practices or beliefs that define the person. Ultimately, we're looking for the person's tipping point. What part of her identity is she ready to fight for?

Under this standard, Deborah Marks's should be an easy case. Yes, she cared about making sales, but her body was hers, and she wasn't going to sacrifice it for the whims of supervisor. She had the requisite training and she could do the job. Only her supervisor's preferences were standing in the way.

To be clear, this is not to say that Marks would automatically have a winning claim. Recognizing the right is only half the inquiry. There is still the question of whether her employer should have accommodated Marks's personality, and this will be the harder side of the equation. Before turning to that question, let me say a few more words about the right to personality.

Not everyone is going to like this. Some will balk at the idea of stretching civil rights law beyond the traditional package of traits. The right to personality, they'll argue, will water down existing protections, making it harder to accomplish the important work of civil rights that still needs to be done. To put a finer point in it, they will argue that hairstyles, piercings, and preferences about make-up are superficial concerns as compared to, say, structural racism or gender bias. And I agree with this. I'm not making a claim about equivalents. I'm not saying that personality is as

serious a thing as a person's race or sex, or that personality discrimination has the same social consequences as racism or sexism. The
point is that difference matters. Civil rights law shouldn't confine
itself to stamping out bias; it should also cultivate authenticity. As
moral compass of American law, civil rights law should embrace
the good as it attacks the bad. It should give a voice to outsiders of
every shape and size. The goal should be to treat everyone better.

Having said that, let me confess that I share the concern about
watering down existing protections. For that reason, think of my
proposal as a bridge, connecting the old civil rights and the new
civil rights. Rather than a wholesale replacement of existing civil
rights law, my proposal should supplement existing doctrine.
Whether this will make a difference, I can't say. But this is one of
those moments where my utopian streak kicks in. Instead of watering down protections, maybe the right to personality will help
beef up existing protections. When it comes to equality, insiders
have all the power. Outsiders must persuade insiders of their
worth. They must demonstrate that their difference shouldn't disqualify them from a good life. Would this be easier if the insiders
had some skin in the game? Maybe insiders need to see that difference is something we all share in common.

Derek Black was born to hate.[23] The son of Don Black, a former
Klan member and founder of the website Stormfront, Derek
grew up in the nerve center of the white nationalist movement.[24]
A bright kid with a knack for technology, Derek developed a
website that sought to teach white nationalism to children. He
was ten at the time. Derek would go on to host a daily radio
show and speak regularly at white nationalism conferences. On
the radio, in speeches, and on Stormfront, Derek promoted the

idea that, because of immigration, America was heading toward a white genocide. White genocide was something that David Duke, Derek's godfather, had been talking about for a long time. Derek made the idea stick. In white nationalist circles, Derek Black was going places. He was the future of the movement. That was until he went to college.

Derek enrolled at New College of Florida, a well-ranked liberal arts college in Sarasota. Although less than four hours from Derek's family in West Palm Beach, New College was like a different planet. At New College, Derek found a diverse community that bent heavily toward progressive politics. Rather than try to change the place, Derek focused on his studies. He was particularly interested in Medieval European history. He didn't abandon his political work. He still hosted his radio show, organized conferences, and posted on Stormfront, but Derek didn't advertise his beliefs. His classmates had no idea who Derek Black really was.

Over time, Derek's life began to change. He became friends with people he otherwise would have never met, including an immigrant from Peru. In a conversation about racism, a student referenced Stormfront. Derek acted as if he wasn't familiar with the site. By then Derek was living two distinct lives. Every weekday morning, he would leave student housing to call in to his radio show. At night, he would hang out and watch zombie movies with his friends, many of whom were members of groups that Derek railed against on his show.

It was only a matter of time before Derek's two lives collided. A student who was doing research about terrorist groups happened upon a picture of Derek. The student posted about his discovery on an active forum for New College students. The post went viral. Derek was busted.

Here's where the story takes an unexpected turn. Derek became an outcast, but only for a short while. As Derek isolated himself from the school community, retreating from a public life on campus, a group of students worked to bring him back into the fold. Rather than expel him, they engaged him. The leader was an Orthodox Jewish student. He invited Derek to Shabbat dinner, and Derek went. And he went back, again and again, until it became a regular part of his life. More students went, and a community developed. They talked. They talked about their lives. They talked about politics. There was mutual respect. They were friends. Eventually, the group didn't shy away from asking Derek about his view on race and identity, and Derek didn't shy away from responding. It was clear that Derek's views had changed. He distanced himself from Stormfront and white nationalism. He studied Jewish scripture, German multiculturalism, and the history of Islam.

After graduation, while staying with his parents in Florida, Derek announced that he was leaving the white nationalism movement. In a statement published by the Southern Poverty Law Center, an organization that keeps tabs on Stormfront and groups like it, Derek apologized for his past actions.[25] "The things I have said as well as my actions have been harmful to people of color, people of Jewish descent, activists striving for opportunity and fairness for all," he wrote.[26] "I am sorry for the damage done."[27] Derek Black has since changed his name. He moved away from Florida to attend graduate school. His relationship with his family is, to put it mildly, rocky.

Derek Black's story is a story about family and ideology. It is a story about rupture and redemption. But, most of all, it is a story about conversation. The students at New College, especially the students who went to all those Shabbat dinners, did a brave thing—they refused to give up on Derek Black. They engaged him. They listened to what Derek had to say, and he responded in kind. At a time when conversation feels like a lost art, when the internet has made it easier to wriggle out of uncomfortable interactions, these young people put in the work. Conversation can't rewrite the past; it can't heal all wounds. But reasons are a powerful thing.

The future of civil rights is accommodation. Opening up, negotiating, finding common ground—accommodation offers a new way of thinking about equality. Rather than treating identity as a standard form, rather than searching in vain for discriminatory intent, rather than squeezing people into boxes, accommodation reorients civil rights law around inclusion. Take people as they come, judge them on their own terms, and try to find balance. The central question in an accommodation case is whether an employer can adapt the workplace to fit the needs of the employee. This is not as one-sided as it sounds, however. Accommodation is a joint venture. Employees must give as well as take. Accommodation spurns rigidity on both sides. It is at its most effective when people work together. The exchange is what matters, the meeting of the minds. Accommodation is a tool for sharing information.

So how will it work? The template, once again, is religious discrimination under Title VII of the Civil Rights Act. There, an employer must take steps to accommodate an employee's religious beliefs or practices.[28] While this may sound like an onerous burden, it is really not. Courts have set a low bar, releasing employers from an obligation to accommodate if doing so would pose an undue hardship. A term of art, undue hardship means more than a *de minimus* cost on the operation of the employer's business, which is a lawyer's way of saying that the employer doesn't have to do much.[29] The reality of religious accommodations, however, is that much of the work is done in the shadows of the law. The accommodation mandate facilitates conversation. Negotiation is a built-in feature. Employees speak up, as do employers. Both sides listen. Each gives reasons. Law cannot be reduced to wins and losses. Accommodation drives parties to resolve conflicts without resorting to litigation. Even if they can't find common ground, at least the parties get the opportunity to explain who they are and what they need. This is no small thing.

Under my proposal, if an employee has a sincere claim about her personality, then the employer's accommodation obligation will kick in. It, too, will be modeled on religious discrimination law, adopting the same basic tests and objectives. The legal status of undue hardship would remain the same, as would the baseline conception of discrimination, namely, the failure to make reasonable accommodations for an employee's personality would give rise to liability. Importantly, the goal is to get people talking, to see if they can work things out together.

To make things less abstract, go back to Deborah Marks, the telemarketer who wanted an outside sales job. Marks made her supervisor aware of her interest in the promotion and he was crystal clear about what she would have to do. "Lose the weight and you'll get promoted," he said.[30] Under my proposal, the legal question is whether that request amounts to discrimination. To answer that question, we need to look at the employer's burden. Specifically, we need to assess the costs of carving out an exception. Would doing so pose an undue hardship? My intuition is that it would not. The stakes in Marks's case are remarkably low. She had a strong sales record, with the accolades to back it up. Sure, employers can have preferences about how their staff present themselves. And this is no doubt a legitimate arena in which an employer may regulate. It just does not seem like accommodating Marks will cost very much. Indeed, if her sales steak continues, it may prove a boon for the employer.

Of course, not everyone will agree with this. The reality is that views about what is reasonable in the land of accommodation vary greatly. And this is a good thing. The law can't guarantee an accommodation for everyone, nor do I want it to. My proposal is not designed to guarantee accommodation for everyone, but rather to make civil rights law a medium for honest conversations about identity. By simply giving outsiders a voice, even if they're asking for too much, the law will ease the ache of difference.

Critics will argue that my proposal is not practical. Specifically, they will argue that it is too costly. Costs come in different flavors. There are the actual costs of accommodation, the money required to adapt to identities. There are the monitoring costs of accommodation, the staffing issues required to keep track of the various accommodations. And there are the procedural costs that would flow from the potential litigation. If everyone has a right to personality, and if everyone avails themselves of that right, then employers and courts will be overwhelmed. It will be the 100-year flood of equality litigation.

My kneejerk reaction is to say that equality is worth it, that there is no such thing as too much equality.[31] But that is not a realistic way of responding to an important concern. Let me suggest instead that there are cost-cutting mechanisms built into my proposal. For starters, most people will not avail themselves of the new system. Though the right to personality may seem boundless at first glance, it will be hard to enjoy the right in practice. Recall that the standard for the right to personality is high. Not just any trait will do. The right to personality will only reach traits that are central to the person's existence, traits that are not just deeply held but constitutive of the person's identity as well. For many of us, there are things that matter to us but are not core to our being. I have a few tattoos, but I wouldn't really care if an employer asked me to cover them up. Frankly, I usually cover them up on my own anyway. For others, by contrast, a tattoo is more than skin deep. Some tattoos are religious in nature. Other tattoos honor a deceased relative or commemorate a significant moment in a person's life. The right to personality draws power from its malleability. Each of us has our own tipping point, our own line in the sand. The law should patrol those points and lines.

Moreover, the accommodation mandate itself should keep costs down. No doubt this sounds absurd, but bear with me. I simply don't anticipate a flood of litigation. Maybe there will be at first, as people are exploring new terrain, but legal norms have a way of taking shape over time. As lawyers and clients come to learn the governing rules, their expectations will adjust accordingly. Once people realize that the standard for accommodation does not favor claimants, they have less incentive to follow through with a lawsuit. But, again, my hope is that lawsuits aren't going to be what drives change under my proposal. Conversation will do the heavy lifting.

Which raises another important question: What if conversation can't fix the problem? What if, even worse, it exacerbates bias? Contact isn't a panacea, and not everyone is moved by reasons. Along this line, a colleague of mine offered the example of an employee who, after she reveals she is transgender, falls out of favor with her employer. She doesn't get fired or transferred or anything official like that, but she struggles to connect with her boss from then on. I countered with an even harder example: Say that the employer objects to her identity on religious grounds. In that case, no amount of conversation may serve to work things out.

There is a larger lesson embedded in this criticism. Civil rights law is hamstrung by its own ambitions. Changing hearts and minds is no small task. Institutions take time to reform. Equality is a life's work. No amount of dolphins jumping on a poster can make people get along. There are always going to be people who don't want to engage, people for whom conversation is not an option.

The threat of conversation doing damage is real. I am particularly concerned about the risk to outsiders who are reluctant to speak out about who they really are. Coming out is always a leap of faith. Ultimately, I believe it is a leap worth taking when the circumstances are right for the person. Each of us has to decide that for ourselves. But my hope is there will be more positive conversations than negative ones, that over time we'll get better at connecting with each other. Difference is the through line; it is the mortar that will hold equality together.

Samantha Elauf loved the mall.[32] The shopping, the movies, the sushi—Woodland Hills Mall in Tulsa, Oklahoma was Samantha Elauf's home away from home.[33] It only made sense for the seventeen-year-old to get a job there, so she applied to work at the children's store owned by Abercrombie & Fitch. For her interview with the store's assistant manager, Elauf wore a black headscarf. The assistant manager rated Elauf qualified to work at the store, but questioned whether the headscarf would be permissible under the company's Look Policy, which deems "caps" as too informal for Abercrombie's image.

Is a headscarf a cap?

Unsure, the assistant manager asked the manager, who likewise didn't know. The assistant manager then asked the district manager, who decided that the headscarf violated the Look Policy. No headwear is allowed, the district manager concluded, not even religious garb. Elauf didn't get the job. She was seventeen at the time.

Elauf never told them that she was Muslim. She never said the headscarf was religious in nature. Abercrombie assumed it was, and it actually was, but Abercrombie didn't know that for sure. In court, after being sued by the Equal Employment Opportunity Commission on Elauf's behalf, Abercrombie argued that it couldn't be liable under the circumstances. If the claimant doesn't ask for an accommodation, how is the company supposed to know to provide one?

I have a certain amount of sympathy for the company's argument. It sort of feels like Elauf didn't advocate for herself at the time, that she didn't speak up when it could have made a difference. But the problem is that speaking up wouldn't have made a difference. The assistant manager assumed that Elauf's headscarf was religious, and the district manager said that not even religious headwear was acceptable under the Look Policy. Which means that actual knowledge wouldn't have made a difference. Elauf wasn't getting this job, and it was because of her religion. So concluded the Supreme Court.[34] In 8-1 decision, the Court said actual knowledge wasn't required.[35] Abercrombie allowed its suspicion about Elauf's religion to affect its decision-making, and that is enough to run afoul of the law.[36]

Note, too, that Elauf's case occupies the squishy ground in between disparate treatment and accommodation. The reason Abercrombie didn't hire Elauf was because it didn't want to accommodate her religious practice. This is important to keep in mind as we consider how my proposal will work in practice. Recall my distinction between old discrimination and new discrimination. Elauf's case is a prime example of new discrimination. Abercrombie wasn't targeting Muslims or women or Muslim women. The case was about how she presented herself, about how she lived her religious identity. The question was whether her identity conflicted with the company's policy against caps.

I'm wary of drawing a hard distinction between disparate treatment and accommodation. While there are surely cases that cleanly fall on one side of the line, new discrimination cases tend to straddle the line. Say an employer fires an employee because she wears her hair in a certain way. This is tantamount to denying the employee an accommodation, as the employer will not make space in the workplace for the employee's hairstyle. A little bit intent and a little bit accommodation. This is a feature of the doctrine, not a shortcoming. I am fully in favor of accommodation creep. The way I see it, the real failure in Samantha Elauf's case was that no one at Abercrombie asked her about her headscarf. They made assumptions about who she is and what she wants. They denied her the opportunity to be heard on the matter. What would have happened had they asked? Would they have dealt with the matter differently?

A little precision is in order. While this book is about civil rights law in general, I have focused specifically on employment discrimination. While I believe my proposal would also work in other domains of civil rights law, such as discrimination in education, housing, and public accommodations, I made a conscious choice to focus on employment. Two considerations drove this decision. The first is that employment discrimination often serves as the model for other areas of civil rights law. As a matter of doctrine, it makes sense to start in the workplace, as it is the most developed area within the field.

The broader reason, however, is that there is something special about employment. Work is something most people have to do. Unless you're a person of independent means, you're going to have to work, and you might not have a lot of control over where, or with whom, you work. Employees are bound together by a common purpose—the good of the employer. Work is a cooperative venture. To be effective, employees have to be able to set aside their differences and do what's best for the business. Work involves sacrifice. When they step into the workplace, employees surrender themselves to the employer, burying certain aspects of their identity. Employment discrimination patrols this negotiation. When does an employer expect its employees to sacrifice more than they should?

Legal scholar Cynthia Estlund's book *Working Together* has been a great influence on my thinking about employment discrimination law and the future of civil rights.[37] Estlund argues that the workplace is uniquely positioned to counteract social forces that are driving Americans apart, forces like residential segregation and the decline of civic organizations. Through their experiences at work, employees form lasting relationships with people they would have otherwise never met. The involuntariness of work is critical. Co-workers are thrust into a setting where they have to get along well enough to do their jobs. Along the way, they learn about each other. They overcome stereotypes and rethink the world around them. The key is that these changes don't stay at work. Employees take them out of the workplace and into their private lives, from where they will spread to their families and friends. Simply put, the workplace is a breeding ground for real, lasting change.

This is why I focus my energies on the workplace, and why I believe the future of civil rights law should start there.

Early in my career, I had the opportunity to attend a talk by a leading legal scholar. The law professor enterprise was still new to me, so I made sure to soak everything in. A seasoned speaker, he exuded casual comfort without relinquishing command of the room. When it came time for questions, the audience banded together to demonstrate their concerns with the speaker's proposal. Each question built on the one before it, snowballing into a sustained critique. Amazingly, the speaker was unfazed, and the audience was captivated. There was no animosity in the room. It was symbiosis. The audience made great points, and the speaker credited each point, acknowledging what it meant for this theory as a whole. No one was trying to win the conversation. He had an idea, and he made a proposal to breathe life into the idea. He couldn't account for every set of facts, and he said so. Toward the end of the talk, in response to a particularly aggressive question, he said something that stuck with me. If the proposal doesn't work, he said, don't reject the idea.

So much of what we do as legal scholars is calibrating ideas and proposals. Striking this balance is never easy. Even for the best projects, the translation stage is the hardest. I am fully aware that my proposal may not work on the ground. Practical considerations often overwhelm aspirations. If the proposal doesn't work, don't reject the idea just yet.

2014 marked the fiftieth anniversary of the Civil Rights Act of 1964. Scholars gathered all over the country to mark this occasion, holding a number of conferences throughout the year. The mood at the conferences I attended was surprising. These weren't celebrations. They were not retrospectives on all the good the Civil Rights Act has done. The mood was darker than that, almost bleak at times. The participants were worried that the law had stalled in its efforts to make change. There was a strong sense, which seemed to be widely shared, that people wanted the law to do more. I know I agree with that sentiment. We are at a critical moment in the arc of equality. What will the future of civil rights look like? How can we better equip our system of righting wrongs to meet the needs of discrimination today?

If nothing else, this book is meant to contribute to that conversation.

Conclusion

In February 2014, Dale Hansen, a sportscaster in Dallas, Texas, delivered an editorial during the sports segment of the nightly news.[1] The topic of "Dale Hansen Unplugged" that night was Michael Sam, a college football standout from the University of Missouri.[2] Sam had come out as gay,[3] and his stock in the approaching National Footbal League draft was plummeting.[4] Hansen quoted NFL officials who said that Sam wouldn't be welcome in NFL locker rooms. The locker room is a man's world, the officials said. Sam's future teammates would be uncomfortable with a gay man in their presence, the officials suggested. Hansen railed against the hypocrisy of it all. Domestic abusers, rapists, drunk drivers, and drug users have all found refuge in NFL locker rooms. But Michael Sam was the problem. He is where players will draw the line.

Hansen's monologue is a plea for tolerance. He strikes a compassionate tone, all the while acknowledging his own biases. "I'm not always comfortable when a man tells me he's gay. I don't understand his world," he said. "But I do understand that he's part of mine." Hansen punctuates his speech with a reference to poet Audre Lorde: "It is not our differences that divide us. It is our inability to recognize, accept, and celebrate those differences."[5]

Hansen couldn't have found a better advocate for accepting difference. Through her writing and activism, Audre Lorde was a powerful voice against racism, sexism, and homophobia. She wrote passionately about illness and bodies and death. She gave voice to outsiders everywhere.

A white male sportscaster defends a black gay football player by marshaling a quote from a black lesbian poet. The contrasts are instructive. However divided we may seem, we share a common humanity. We shouldn't be surprised by Dale Hansen's support for Michael Sam. Nor should we be surprised by his embrace of a queer black protest poet. People have a phenomenal capacity for acceptance.

Civil rights law has been a transformative force in our law and culture. It is a beacon of change, a testament to the power of law to change the way people live their lives. But the work of civil rights is never done. Equality is a moving target. Bias doesn't just linger; it adapts. In its current formulation, civil rights law is geared to contend with a particular flavor of discrimination. So long as the discrimination is aimed at status, so long as group membership is the lynchpin of the enterprise, civil rights law is well-suited to the task. When the discrimination is about performance, when it is about self-definition or constraints on how we live our lives, when it is aimed at the one thing that sets the person apart from everyone else, civil rights law is lost at sea. The time has come to rethink the way we do equality. Difference is the path forward.

When he was in fifth grade, my son was diagnosed with inattentive-type ADHD. For all his smarts, he struggles with organization. He'll do his assignments, and he'll do them well, but he doesn't always turn them in. His backpack is like a black hole. His teachers thought he didn't care about his work. They thought he was being difficult. We were really hard on him, too. As a parent, it's not easy to watch a smart kid struggle in school. Once we listened to him—really heard what he had to say—it was clear that he did care, very much so. It wasn't defiance; it was shame. He wanted to do better.

The key to his success is a little light prodding—check the assignment notebook, remind him about his upcoming assignments, a quick check-in so he doesn't get distracted. These are flashes, brief moments in his teachers' day. When he stays on task, he does wonderfully. And it's not just on his teachers. He has rules to follow—rules about his assignment notebook, rules about asking for feedback. We do our part, too. His future is a group effort. Small interventions make a huge difference.

He's older now. His life is more complicated than it used to be, and his views on issues of equality have become muddier, too. The transition from child to adulthood is fraught even under the best of circumstances, and I simply can't wrap my mind around what it's like to come of age in a time of social media and endless cable news. The dilemma of parenting a teenager is how to control the cocoon. Eventually they emerge on their own, and then you watch to see who they will become.

I asked him about the "Work Together" song, if he remembered it, how it made him feel. Mostly embarrassed, he said. He clearly didn't want to have this conversation. Teenagers. When I asked him what song he would write today, he got quiet. After a moment, he said, "I don't know."

It's a work in progress. We'll keep talking about it.

NOTES

INTRODUCTION

1. Eun Kyung Kim, *Sister Who Shaved Head in Solidarity Told to Wear Wig at Work*, TODAY, June 17, 2013, *at* http://www.today.com/news/sister-who-shaved-head-solidarity-told-wear-wig-work-6C10345060.
2. *Id.*
3. *Bald and Beautiful: Spokane Hairstylist Chooses Family Over Her Job*, NBC RIGHT NOW, KNDO/KNDU, *at* http://www.nbcrightnow.com/story/22612188/bald-and-beautiful-spokane-hairstylist-chooses-family-over-her-job.
4. Kim, *Sister Who Shaved Head, supra* note 1.
5. ANDREW SOLOMON, FAR FROM THE TREE: PARENTS, CHILDREN AND THE SEARCH FOR IDENTITY 4 (2012).
6. Chenzira v. Cincinnati Children's Hospital Medical Center, No. 1:11-CV-00917, 2012 WL 6721098 (S.D. Ohio, Dec. 27, 2012).
7. Cloutier v. Costco Wholesale Corp., 390 F.3d 126 (1st Cir. 2004).
8. Peterson v. Minidoka, 118 F.3d 1351 (9th Cir. 1997).
9. Rodriguez v. City of Chicago, 156 F.3d 771 (7th Cir. 1998).
10. EEOC v. Abercrombie & Fitch Stores, Inc. (Abercrombie & Fitch I), No. 4:08CV1470 JCH, 2009 WL 3517578, (E.D. Mo. Oct. 26, 2009); EEOC v. Abercrombie & Fitch Stores, Inc. (Abercrombie & Fitch II), No. 4:08CV1470 JCH, 2009 WL 3517584 (E.D. Mo. Oct. 26, 2009).

CHAPTER 1

1. The following comes from *Price Waterhouse v. Hopkins*, 490 U.S. 228 (1989).

2. *A Solid Investment: Making Use of the Nation's Human Capital*, FEDERAL GLASS CEILING COMMISSION, Nov. 1995, *at* https://www.dol.gov/oasam/programs/history/reich/reports/ceiling2.pdf.

3. City of L.A. Dep't of Water & Power v. Manhart, 435 U.S. 702 (1978).

4. Biography of Sandra Day O'Connor, SANDRA DAY O'CONNOR INSTITUTE, *at* http://oconnorinstitute.org/programs/oconnor-history/sandra-day-oconnor-library-and-archives/biography/.

5. The official name of the law school where I work is the Sandra Day O'Connor College of Law at Arizona State University. *See* http://www.law.asu.edu. The school took Justice O'Connor's name in 2006. Adam Kress, *ASU Law to Be Named for Sandra Day O'Connor*, PHOENIX BUSINESS J., April 5, 2006, *at* http://www.bizjournals.com/phoenix/stories/2006/04/03/daily41.html.

6. Wal-Mart Stores, Inc. v. Dukes, 564 U.S. 338 (2011).

7. Doug Altner, *Why Do 1.4 Million Americans Work at Walmart, With Many More Trying To?* FORBES, Nov. 27, 2013, *at* https://www.forbes.com/sites/realspin/2013/11/27/why-do-1-4-million-americans-work-at-walmart-with-many-more-trying-to/#719655eee599.

8. Henry Blodget, *Walmart Employs 1% of America. Should It Be Forced to Pay Its Employees More?* BUSINESS INSIDER, Sept. 20, 2010, *at* http://www.businessinsider.com/walmart-employees-pay.

9. A particularly helpful source on the statistics in the Wal-Mart litigation is Melissa Hart, *Learning from Wal-Mart*, 10 EMPLOYEE RTS. & EMP. POL'Y J. 355 (2006–2007).

10. Plaintiffs' Motion for Class Certification and Memorandum of Points and Authorities at 25, Dukes et al. v. Wal-Mart Stores, Inc., 222 F.R.D. 137 (No. C01-02252 MJJ) [hereinafter Plaintiffs' Motion for Class].

11. *Id.*

12. *Id.*

13. *Id.*

14. Hart, *Learning, supra* note 9, at 364 (citing motion for certification).

15. Cora Daniels, *Women v. Wal-Mart: How Can the Retailer Reconcile Its Storied Culture with the Anger of These Female Workers?* FORTUNE, July 21, 2003, at http://archive.fortune.com/magazines/fortune/fortune_archive/2003/07/21/346130/index.htm.

16. Daniels, *Women v. Wal-Mart, supra* note 15.

17. *Id.*

18. *Id.*

19. *Id.*

20. Wal-Mart Stores, Inc. v. Dukes, 564 U.S. 338, 349–352 (2011).

21. *Dukes,* 564 U.S. at 351–352.

22. KENJI YOSHINO, COVERING: THE HIDDEN ASSAULT ON OUR CIVIL RIGHTS 22 (2006).

23. *See* ERVING GOFFMAN, THE PRESENTATION OF SELF IN EVERY DAY LIFE (1959).

24. Jespersen v. Harrah's Operating Co., 444 F.3d 1104 (9th Cir. 2006) (en banc).

25. *Id.* at 1108.

26. *Id.* at 1108.

27. *Id.* at 1107.

28. *Id.* at 1107.

29. *Id.* at 1107.

30. *Id.* at 1107.

31. *Id.* at 1109–1111, 1112–1113.

32. *Id.* at 1113.

33. *Id.* at 1112.

34. What follows is my own take on *Jespersen.* To be clear, there are compelling scholarly accounts that come down differently on the case. *See, e.g.,* Michael Selmi, *The Many Faces of Darlene Jespersen,* 14 DUKE J. GENDER L. & POL. 467 (2007); Meredith M. Render, 22 YALE J.L. & FEMINISM 133(2010); Devon Carbado et al., *The Jespersen Story: Makeup and Women at Work, in* EMPLOYMENT DISCRIMINATION STORIES 105 (Joel Wm. Friedman ed., 2006).

35. The following comes from Nelson v. James H. Knight DDS, P.C., 834 N.W.2d 64 (Iowa 2013).

36. *Nelson,* 834 N.W. 2d at 67.

37. *Id.* at 70.

38. *Id.* at 70.

39. Nelson v. James H. Knight DDS, P.C., No. 11–1857, 2012 WL 6652747 (Sup Ct. of Iowa), *withdrawn and superseded by* Nelson v. James H. Knight DDS, P.C., 834 N.W.2d 64 (Iowa).

40. Michael Kimmel, *Fired for Being Beautiful,* N.Y. TIMES (Op-ed), July 16, 2013, at A25.

41. Naomi Wolf, *Through the Lookism Glass,* PROJECT SYNDICATE, July 31, 2013, *at* https://www.project-syndicate.org/commentary/women-s-appearance-and-workplace-sexism-by-naomi-wolf.

42. Pepper Schwartz, *Fired Because a Man Can't Control Himself*, CNN, July 16, 2013, *at* http://www.cnn.com/2013/07/16/opinion/schwartz-fired-looks/index.html?iref=allsearch.

43. Erin Alberty, *Employee's Suit: Company Used Waterboarding to Motivate Workers*, THE SALT LAKE TRIBUNE, February 27, 2008, *at* http://archive.sltrib.com/story.php?ref=/ci_8385103.

44. ANN BRANIGAR HOPKINS, SO ORDERED: MAKING PARTNER THE HARD WAY (1996).

45. Price Waterhouse v. Hopkins, 490 U.S. 228, 250–252 (1989).

46. *Id.* at 258.

47. *Id.* at 235.

48. *Id.* at 235.

49. *Id.* at 235–236.

50. *Id.* at 256.

51. *Id.* at 250.

52. *Id.* at 251.

53. ERVING GOFFMAN, STIGMA: NOTES ON THE MANAGEMENT OF SPOILED IDENTITY (1963).

54. YOSHINO, COVERING, *supra* note 22, at ix.

55. The text of the speech, also called the "How Long, Not Long" speech, is available at Dr. Martin Luther King, Jr., *Our God Is Marching On!*, THE MARTIN LUTHER KING, JR. RESEARCH AND EDUCATION INSTITUTE AT STANFORD UNIVERSITY (delivered on March 25, 1965), *at* https://kinginstitute.stanford.edu/our-god-marching.

56. King, Jr., *Our God Is Marching On!*, *supra* note 55.

57. 347 U.S. 483 (1954).

58. 438 U.S. 265 (1978).

59. 539 U.S. 558 (2003).

60. King, Jr., *Our God Is Marching On!*, *supra* note 55.

61. HOPKINS, SO ORDERED, *supra* note 44, at 385.

62. *Id.* at 279–80.

63. Ann Hopkins, Price Waterhouse v. Hopkins: *A Personal Account of a Sexual Discrimination Plaintiff*, 22 HOFSTRA LAB. & EMP. L.J. 357 (2005).

64. *Id.* at 413.

65. *Id.* at 414.

CHAPTER 2

1. Etsitty v. Utah Transit Authority, 502 F.3d 1215 (10th Cir. 2007) (hereinafter Etsitty II).

2. Etsitty v. Utah Transit Authority, No. 2:04CV616 DS, 2005 WL 1505610 (D. Utah, June 25, 2005) [hereinafter Etsitty I].

3. The following discussion relies heavily on the work of leading critical race theorist Cheryl Harris. *See* Cheryl I. Harris, *Whiteness as Property*, 106 Harv. L. Rev. 1707 (1992–1993).

4. People v. Dean, 14 Mich. 406 (1866).

5. *Id.* at 414.

6. *Id.* at 424–425.

7. State v. Chavers, 50 Jones (NC) 11 (1857).

8. *Chavers*, 50 Jones (NC) at 12–13.

9. State v. Bd. of Dir. School Dist. 16, Montgomery City, 242 S.W. 545 (Ark. 1922).

10. *Id.* at 546.

11. My introduction to the *Rhinelander* case came from Angela Onwuachi-Willig's wonderful book, *According to Our Hearts:* Rhinelander v. Rhinelander *and the Law of the Multiracial Family* (Yale 2013). The following discussion draws on Onwuachi-Willig's book.

12. Complaint at 3, Etsitty v. Utah Transit Authority I, 2005 WL 150561 (D. Utah, June 24, 2005).

13. *Id.*

14. *Id.*

15. *Id*

16. Complaint at 4, Etsitty v. Utah Transit Authority I, 2005 WL 150561 (D. Utah, June 24, 2005).

17. Etsitty II, 502 F.3d 1215, 1219 (10th Cir. 2007).

18. *Id.* at 1219.

19. David Haldene, *Vegetarian Bus Driver Has a Beef with Burger Offer*, Los Angeles Times, June 6, 1996, *at* http://articles.latimes.com/1996-06-06/news/mn-12324_1_bus-driver.

20. I stole this joke. It was too good to pass up. *See id.*

21. *Id.*

22. David Haldene, *Vegetarian Bus Driver Settles Suit Against Agency for $50,000*, Los Angeles Times, Nov. 20, 1996, at http://articles.latimes.com/1996-11-20/news/mn-992_1_bus-driver.

23. *Id.*

24. *Taco Bell Pays $27,000 to Settle Religious Discrimination Lawsuit*, Huffington Post, May 1, 2012, at http://www.huffingtonpost.com/2012/04/30/taco-bell-religious-discrimination-lawsuit_n_1465590.html.

25. Press Release, U.S. Equal Employment Opportunity Commission, Lawrence Transportation Systems to Pay $30,000 to Settle EEOC

Religious Discrimination Lawsuit (August 16, 2011), at https://www1. eeoc.gov//eeoc/newsroom/release/8-16-11f.cfm?renderforprint=1.

26. Stacy Teicher Khadaroo, *Sikh Woman Wins Settlement from US Government over Wearing Religious Knife*, CHRISTIAN SCIENCE MONITOR, Nov. 6, 2014, at http://www.csmonitor.com/USA/Justice/2014/1106/Sikh-woman-wins-settlement-from-US-government-over-wearing-religious-knife.

27. Minersville School District v. Gobits, 310 U.S. 586 (1940).

28. Church of the Lukumi Babalu Aye v. City of Hialeah, 508 U.S. 520 (1993).

29. Reynolds v. United States, 98 U.S. 145 (1878).

30. Lemon v. Kurtzman, 403 U.S. 602 (1971).

31. ANDREW SOLOMON, FAR FROM THE TREE: PARENTS, CHILDREN AND THE SEARCH FOR IDENTITY (2012).

32. AMERICAN PSYCHIATRIC ASSOCIATION, DIAGNOSTIC AND STATISTICAL MANUAL OF MENTAL DISORDERS (DSM-5) (2013).

33. 29 C.F.R. 1603.3(d)(1) ("Disability does not include transvestitism, transsexualism, pedophilia, exhibitionism, voyeurism, gender identity disorders not resulting from physical impairments, or sexual behavior disorders").

34. Ulane v. Eastern Airlines, Inc., 742 F.2d 1081 (7th Cir. 1984).

35. Etsitty v. Utah Transit Auth., 502 F.3d 1215, 1220–1222 (10th Cir. 2007).

36. *Ulane*, 742 F.2d at 1084–1085, 1086–1087.

37. I detail this story at length, in Zachary A. Kramer, *The New Sex Discrimination*, 63 DUKE L.J. 891, 910–911 (2014).

38. Cary Franklin, *Inventing the "Traditional Concept" of Sex Discrimination*, 125 HARV. L. REV. 1307 (2012).

39. JESS ROW, YOUR FACE IN MINE: A NOVEL (2014).

40. *Id.* at 41–42, 261.

41. *Id.* at 27.

42. *Id.* at 33.

43. *Id.* at 36.

44. *Id.* at 36.

45. 42 U.S.C. § 12102(1)(A)–(B) ("The Term disability means, with respect to an individual (A) a physical or mental impairment that substantially limits one or more major life activities of such individual; (B) a record of such an impairment").

46. 42 U.S.C. § 12102(1)(C) ("The Term disability means, with respect to an individual (C) being regarded as having such an impairment").

47. *See* McDonnell Douglas Corp. v. Green, 411 U.S. 792 (1973) (establishing a three-tiered burden-shifting scheme to establish discrimination under Title VII).

48. St. Mary's Honor Center v. Hicks, 509 U.S. 502 (1993); Texas Dep't of Community Affairs v. Burdine, 450 U.S. 248 (1981).

49. SOLOMON, FAR FROM THE TREE, *supra* note 31.

CHAPTER 3

1. Dawson v. Bumble & Bumble, 398 F.3d 211 (2d Cir. 2005) [hereinafter Dawson II].

2. *Id.* at 213.

3. Dawson v. Bumble & Bumble, 246 F. Supp. 2d 301, 318 (2003) [hereinafter Dawson I].

4. *Id.*

5. *Dawson II*, 398 F.3d at 214.

6. *Dawson I*, 246 F. Supp. 2d at 309.

7. *Dawson II*, 398 F.3d at 215.

8. *Dawson II*, 398 F.3d at 215.

9. *Dawson II*, 398 F.3d at 215–216.

10. New York State Human Rights Law, N.Y. EXEC. LAW § 290 et seq. She also sued under New York City's corresponding nondiscrimination ordinance. New York City Human Rights Law, N.Y.C. ADMIN CODE, Title 8.

11. *Dawson II*, 398 F.3d at 225; *Dawson I*, 246 F. Supp. 2d at 330.

12. *Dawson II*, 398 F.3d at 218 (quoting Simonton v. Runyon, 232 F.3d 33, 38 (2d Cir. 2000)).

13. Shaw v. Citicorp Credit Services, 35 TRIALS DIGEST 34, 1994 WL 851348 (N.D. Cal.) (Verdict and Settlement Summary).

14. *Id.*

15. Elliot Spagat, Associated Press, *San Diego Cabbies Cry Foul over Body Odor Test*, USA TODAY, at http://www.usatoday.com/story/money/business/2014/09/13/san-diego-cabbies-cry-foul-over-body-odor-test/15576207/.

16. Jerry Seinfeld, I'm Telling You for the Last Time (Aug. 9, 1998). The video of Seinfeld's performance can be seen here: https://www.youtube.com/watch?v=bsAl0OxDxOA.

17. *See, e.g.*, Vickers v. Fairfield Med. Ctr., 453 F.3d 757, 763 (6th Cir. 2006); Hamm v. Weyauwega Milk Prods., Inc., 332 F.3d 1058, 1062–1065 (7th

Cir. 2003); King v. Super Serv., Inc., 68 F. App'x 659, 660–664 (6th Cir. 2003); Simonton, 232 F.3d at 35; Spearman v. Ford Motor Co., 231 F.3d 1080, 1085 (7th Cir. 2000); Higgins v. New Balance Athletic Shoe, Inc., 194 F.3d 252, 259–261 (1st Cir. 1999); Desantis v. Pac. Tel. & Tel. Co., 608 F.2d 327, 332 (9th Cir. 1974). Things might be changing on this front, however. The U.S. Court of Appeals for the Seventh Circuit recently held that sexual orientation is protected under Title VII. *See* Hively v. Ivy Tech Community College of Indiana, No. 3:14-cv-1791 (7th Cir. April 4, 2017) (slip opinions). This creates a circuit split, as the Second Circuit recently sided with the majority of courts on this question. *See* Christiansen v. Omnicom Group, Inc., No. 16-748 (2d Cir., March 27, 2017) (slip opinion). It's possible this issue is heading to the Supreme Court.

18. EVE KOSOFSKY SEDGWICK, EPISTEMOLOGY OF THE CLOSET 25–26 (1990).

19. Dawson v. Bumble & Bumble, 398 F.3d 211, 215 (2d Cir. 2005).

20. 413 F. Supp. 142 (E.D. Mo. 1976).

21. Law professor Kimberlé Crenshaw sparked a widespread conversation about identity with her work on intersectionality. *See* Kimberlé Crenshaw, *Demarginalizing the Intersection of Race and Sex: A Black Feminist Critique of Antidiscrimination Doctrine, Feminist Theory, and Antiracist Politics*, 1989 U. CHI. LEGAL F. 139, 140 ("Because the intersectional experience is greater than the sum of racism and sexism, any analysis that does not take intersectionality into account cannot sufficiently address the particular manner in which Black women are subordinated."); Kimberlé Crenshaw, *Mapping the Margins: Intersectionality, Identity Politics, and Violence Against Women of Color*, 43 STAN. L. REV. 1241, 1244 (1991) ("[T]he intersection of racism and sexism factors into Black women's lives in ways that cannot be captured wholly by looking at the race or gender dimensions of those experiences separately.").

22. *DeGraffenreid*, 413 F. Supp. at 143 (internal quotations omitted).

23. *Id.* at 145.

24. *Id.*

25. DOUGLAS R. HOFSTADTER, LE TON BEAU DE MAROT: IN PRAISE OF THE MUSIC OF LANGUAGE (1997).

26. *Radiolab: Translation*, WNYC (Oct. 20, 2014) (downloaded using iTunes).

27. *Id.*

28. *Id.*

29.   Burrage v. Fedex Freight, Inc., No. 4:10CV2755, 2012 WL 1068794 (N.D. Ohio, March 29, 2012).

30.   *Id.* at *1.

31.   *Id.*

32.   *See* D. Wendy Greene, *Categorically Black, White or Wrong: "Misperception Discrimination" and the State of Title VII Protection*, 47 MICH. J.L. REF. 101 (2013). But this might be changing, at least according to a new paper. *See* Elizabeth E. Aronson, Note, *Perceived-As Plaintiffs: Expanding Title VII Coverage to Discrimination Based on Erroneous Perception*, 67 CASE W. L. REV. 235 (2016).

33.   Americans with Disabilities Act, 42 U.S.C. § 12102(1)(C) ("The Term disability means, with respect to an individual (C) being regarded as having such an impairment").

34.   Darcy v. City of New York, No. 06-2246, 2011 WL 841370 (E.D.N.Y., March 6, 2012).

35.   Equality Act of 1974, H.R. 14752 (93rd Congress, introduced May 14, 1974). Information about the act can be found at http://www.govtrack. us/congress/bills/93/hr14752.

36.   Employment Nondiscrimination Act of 2013, S.B. 815 (113th Congress, introduced April 25, 2013). Information about the bill can be found at https://www.congress.gov/bill/113th-congress/senate-bill/815.

37.   *See* Laura Meckler, *Religious Exemption at Center of ENDA Debate*, WALL ST. J., Nov. 1, 2013, at https://blogs.wsj.com/washwire/2013/11/ 01/religious-exemptions-at-center-of-enda-debate/.

38.   Felicia R. Lee, *After the "White Lie" Implodes, A Rich Narrative Unfurls: "Little White Lie," Lacey Schwartz's Film About Self-Discovery*, N.Y. TIMES, Aug. 1, 2014.

39.   Rebecca Spence, *Documentary Reveals Jewish Mother's "Little White Lie,"* THE TIMES OF ISRAEL, Aug. 17, 2014, at http://www.timesofisrael. com/documentary-reveals-jewish-mothers-little-white-lie/.

40.   Lee, *After the "White Lie" Implodes, supra* note 38.

41.   LITTLE WHITE LIE (Truth Aid 2014).

42.   GenderPAC National News, Interview with Dawn Dawson, at https:// groups.google.com/forum/#!topic/bit.listserv.gaynet/9dbTO7V0Rnc.

43.   *Id.*

44.   *Id.*

45.   *Id.*

46.   *Id.*

47.   *Id.*

CHAPTER 4

1. *See* PGA Tour, Inc. v. Martin, 532 U.S. 661 (2001)

2. Technically, under the Q-School hard card, carts were permitted in the first two rounds. They were not permitted in the third and final round, however.

3. *Martin*, 532 U.S. at 670–671.

4. *Id.* at 668.

5. *Id.* at 669.

6. Jacobellis v. Ohio, 378 U.S. 184, 197 (1964) (Stewart, J., concurring).

7. COMPARATIVE EQUALITY AND ANTI-DISCRIMINATION LAW: CASES, CODES, CONSTITUTIONS, AND COMMENTARY (Oppenheimer, Foster & Han eds., 1st ed., 2012), at 1.

8. 42 U.S.C. § 2000e–2(e).

9. Dothard v. Rawlinson, 433 U.S. 321 (1977)

10. Healey v. Southwood Psychiatric Hosp., 78 F.3d 128 (3d Cir. 1996).

11. Hooters has a record of settling with male claimants who charge the restaurant chain of sex discrimination in hiring. *See* Associated Press, *Hooters Settles Suit by Men Denied Jobs*, N.Y. TIMES, Oct. 1, 1997, at http://www.nytimes.com/1997/10/01/us/hooters-settles-suit-by-men-denied-jobs.html; *Texas Man Settles Discrimination Lawsuit Against Hooters for Not Hiring Male Waiters*, FOX NEWS, April 21, 2009, at http://www.foxnews.com/story/2009/04/21/texas-man-settles-discrimination-lawsuit-against-hooters-for-not-hiring-male.html.

12. For an extensive discussion, see Ann McGinley, *Babes and Beefcakes: Exclusive Hiring Arrangements and Sexy Dressing Codes*, 14 DUKE J. GENDER L. & POL'Y 257 (2007).

13. Davis v. Baltimore Hebrew Congregation, 985 F. Supp. 2d 701 (D. Md. 2013).

14. EEOC v. Exxon Mobile Corp., No. 13-10164, 560 Fed. Appx. 282 (5th Cir. March 25, 2014).

15. PGA Tour v. Martin 532 U.S. 661, 670–671 n.13 (2001).

16. *Id.* at 670–671 n.14.

17. *Id.* at 670–671 n.15.

18. ROBERT C. POST, PREJUDICIAL APPEARANCES: THE LOGIC OF AMERICAN ANTIDISCRIMINATION LAW (2000)

19. Id. at 14.

20. Regents of the University of California v. Bakke, 438 U.S. 265, 407 (1978) (Blackmun, J., concurring).

21. Rivka Galchen, *An Unlikely Ballerina: The Rise of Misty Copeland*, THE NEW YORKER, Sept. 22, 2014, at http://www.newyorker.com/magazine/2014/09/22/unlikely-ballerina.

22.   *Id.*

23.   Michael Cooper, *Misty Copeland Is Promoted to Principal Dancer at American Ballet Theater*, N.Y. TIMES, June 30, 2015, https://www. nytimes.com/2015/07/01/arts/dance/misty-copeland-is-promoted-to-principal-dancer-at-american-ballet-theater.html.

24.   Under Armour, "I Will What I Want" (published July 30, 2014). The commercial can be viewed here: https://www.youtube.com/ watch?v=ZY0cdXr_1MA. As of this writing, the ad has just shy of 11 million views.

25.   MISTY COPELAND, LIFE IN MOTION: AN UNLIKELY BALLERINA (2014).

26.   60 Minutes: Misty Copeland (CBS News May 10, 2015), at http://www. cbsnews.com/news/misty-copeland-unlikely-ballerina-60-minutes/.

27.   FROZEN (Walt Disney Studios 2013).

28.   *See* Coleman v. B–G Maint. Mgmt. of Colo., Inc. 108 F.3d 1199, 1203 (10th Cir. 1997) (quoting Lex K. Larson, EMPLOYMENT DISCRIMINATION § 40.04 (2d ed. 1996)).

29.   PGA Tour, Inc. v Martin, 532 U.S. 661, 705 (2001) (Scalia, J., dissenting).

30.   *Id.* at 705 (Scalia, J., dissenting).

31.   KURT VONNEGUT, JR., *Harrison Bergeron, in* WELCOME TO THE MONKEY HOUSE: A COLLECTION OF SHORT WORKS 7 (1968).

32.   *Id.* at 9.

33.   Anderson v. U.S.F. Logistics (IMC), Inc., 274 F.3d 470 (7th Cir. 2001).

34.   *Id.* at 475–477.

35.   BLACK'S LAW DICTIONARY 536 (6th ed. 1990). Full disclosure, I'm cheating. This is an out-of-date edition of *Black's*. The current edition defines equality in this way: "The quality, state, or condition of being equal; *esp.*, likeness in power or political status." The new definition does little to clarify the concept, as the dictionary doesn't define the term "equal."

36.   Jeffrey Martin, *Casey Martin's Golf Cart Sparks Controversy Again*, USA TODAY SPORTS, June 25, 2013, at http://www.usatoday.com/ story/sports/golf/2013/06/25/casey-martin-golf-cart-oregon-us-golf-association/2458135/.

37.   Cassie Stein, *Martin Claims Discrimination After Cart Revoked*, GOLFWEEK, July 1, 2013, at http://golfweek.com/news/2013/jun/25/ casey-martin-denied-cart-usga/.

38.   *Id.*.

CHAPTER 5

1. The following comes from three sources. *See* Grace Notes, *Suit Revived for Veteran Lifeguard, 66, Who Refused to Wear a Speedo*, N.Y. TIMES, July 24, 2016, at https://www.nytimes.com/2016/07/25/nyregion/suit-revived-for-veteran-lifeguard-66-who-refused-to-wear-a-speedo.html; Thomas Zambito, *Lifeguard, 61, Sues State for Firing Him After He Refused to Wear Speedo*, N.Y. DAILY NEWS, Aug. 18, 2011, at http://www.nydailynews.com/new-york/lifeguard-61-sues-state-firing-refused-wear-speedo-article-1.948776; *This American Life*, WBEZ (Aug. 12, 2016) (downloaded using iTunes).

2. *This American Life*, WBEZ (Aug. 12, 2016) (downloaded using iTunes).

3. *Id.*

4. Zambito, *Lifeguard, 61, supra* note 1.

5. Notes, *Suit Revived, supra* note 1.

6. The story, and quotes, come from German Lopez, *The Most Heartwarming Story You'll Ever Hear About a T.S.A. Pat-Down*, Vox, Aug. 6, 2016, at https://www.vox.com/2016/8/6/12389484/tsa-transgender-gender-nonconforming.

7. *Id.*

8. *Id.*

9. Lindsey Deaton, *Travel Can Be Traumatic for Transgender People*, CINCINNATI.COM, Aug. 5, 2016, at http://www.cincinnati.com/story/opinion/contributors/2016/08/05/travel-can-traumatic-transgender-people/88001924/.

10. *Id.*

11. *Id.*

12. Dawn Ennis, *Her Tweets Tell One Trans Woman's TSA Horror* Story, ADVOCATE, Sept. 22, 2015, at http://www.advocate.com/transgender/2015/9/22/one-trans-womans-tsa-horror-story.

13. Margarita Noriega, *Transgender Woman Live-Tweets Her Expulsion from Orlando Airport*, Vox, Sept. 22, 2015, at https://www.vox.com/2015/9/21/9367327/transgender-shadi-petosky-twitter-orlando-airport.

14. *Id.*

15. Michael Rietmulder, *Transgender Woman Shadi Petosky Live Tweets TSA Nightmare*, Sept. 22, 2015, at http://www.citypages.com/news/transgender-woman-shadi-petosky-live-tweets-tsa-nightmare-7684915.

16. Katie Rogers, *T.S.A. Defends Treatment of Transgender Air Traveler*, N.Y. TIMES, Sept. 22, 2015, at http://www.nytimes.com/2015/09/23/us/shadi-petosky-tsa-transgender.html.

17. *Id.*
18. Trans World Airlines, Inc. v. Hardison, 432 U.S. 63 (1977); *see also* Ansonia Bd. of Educ. v. Philbrook, 479 U.S. 60 (1986) (holding that an employer does not have to accept the employee's proposal for an accommodation).
19. 29 C.F.R. § 16320.2(p) (defining undue hardship as "significant difficulty or expense incurred by a covered entity"). This is a fact-dependent inquiry, depending on the needs of the employee, as well as the circumstances of the employer. The cited regulation also lists a series of factors to consider in making this determination, which includes the nature and cost of accommodation; the overall financial resources of the covered entity; and the impact of the accommodation on the facility. The bottom line is that this is a more stringent standard than undue hardship under Title VII's religious discrimination provision.
20. Order Granting Mot. Dismiss, Lester v. New York State Office of Parks, Recreation & Historic Preservation, No. 10863/09 (N.Y. Sup. Ct. Jan. 20, 2010). Special thanks to Beth DeFelice for her help locating this document.
21. Lester v. New York State Office of Parks, Recreation & Historic Preservation, 32 N.Y.S.3d 225 (N.Y. App. Div., 2016).
22. *Id.* at 228.
23. McDonnell Douglas Corp. v. Green, 411 U.S. 792 (1973). The operative case in New York, where Lester's case is underway, is *Forrest v. Jewish Guild for the Blind*, 819 N.E.2d 988, 1015 (N.Y. 2004) (noting that New York state and city laws follow the *McDonnell Douglas* burden-shifting framework from Title VII jurisprudence).
24. *Lester*, 32 N.Y.S.3d at 228.
25. *This American Life, supra* note 1.
26. Barbara Bradley Hagerty, *Controversy Erupts over Sex-Segregated Brooklyn Bus*, NPR, Oct. 20, 2011, at https://www.npr.org/2011/10/20/141559320/controversy-erupts-over-sex-segregated-brooklyn-bus.
27. *Id.*
28. Metropolitan Transit Authority, Brooklyn Bus Schedules, *at* http://web.mta.info/nyct/service/bus/bklnsch.htm.
29. Michelle Young, *NYC's B-110 Bus Operates Only Within Hasidic Jewish Areas of Brooklyn*, UNTAPPED CITIES, May 3, 2016, *at* https://untappedcities.com/2016/05/03/nycs-b110-bus-operates-only-within-hasidic-jewish-areas-of-brooklyn/.
30. Sam Weis, *What's the Deal with the MTA's Mystery Bus, the All-Hasidic B-110*, BROKELYN.COM, March 2, 2017, *at* https://brokelyn.com/welcome-to-the-magical-mystery-bus-tour/.

31. Joseph Berger, *Out of Enclaves, a Pressure to Accommodate Traditions*, N.Y. Times, Aug. 21, 2013, *at* http://www.nytimes.com/2013/08/22/nyregion/hasidic-jews-turn-up-pressure-on-city-to-accommodate-their-traditions.html.

32. *Id.*

33. Josh Nathan-Kazis, *Hasidic Single-Sex Swimming Sparks New Clash with New York Law—at Local Pool*, Forward, June 1, 2016, *at* https://forward.com/news/341742/hasidic-single-sex-swimming-sparks-new-clash-with-new-york-law-at-the-local/

34. Joseph Berger, *supra* note 31.

35. Isabel Kershner, *She Was Asked to Change Seats. Now She's Charging El Al with Sexism*, N.Y. Times, Feb. 26, 2016), *at https://www.nytimes.com/2016/02/27/world/middleeast/woman-81-to-sue-israeli-airline-over-seat-switch.html* (citing the opinion of preeminent Orthodox scholar Rabbi Moshe Feinstein, who concluded that incident contact on transportation is acceptable if it isn't accompanied by sexual intent). The Kershner piece presents a similar story of incidental contact on transportation, involving the Israeli airline El Al, whose flight attendants asked a woman to move her seat because an Orthodox refused to sit next to her in his assigned seat. For more on the issue of Orthodox Jews interacting with non-Jews in public, including Rabbi Feinstein's thinking on the issue, see Ari Wasserman, Workplace Halacha, *The Rush Hour Crush: Commuting by Public Transportation, at http://www.workplacehalacha.com/wp-content/uploads/2014/05/Chapter-13-Commuting.pdf.*

36. EEOC v. Abercrombie & Fitch Stores, Inc. (Abercrombie & Fitch I), No. 4:08CV1470 JCH, 2009 WL 3517578 (E.D. Mo. Oct. 26, 2009); EEOC v. Abercrombie & Fitch Stores, Inc. (Abercrombie & Fitch II), No. 4:08CV1470 JCH, 2009 WL 3517584 (E.D. Mo. Oct. 26, 2009).

37. Defendants' Memorandum in Opposition to Plaintiff's Motion in Limine at 2, Abercrombie & Fitch I, 2009 WL 351578 (No. 4:08CV1470 JCH), 2009 WL 4900167.

38. Memorandum in Support of Defendants' Motion for Summary Judgment at 5, Abercrombie & Fitch I, 2009 WL 351578 (No. 4:08CV1470 JCH), 2009 WL 2565188.

39. Plaintiff's Trial Brief at 2, Abercrombie & Fitch I, 2009 WL 351578 (No. 4:08CV1470 JCH), 2009 WL 4900158.

40. Abercrombie & Fitch I, 2009 WL 351578, at *1.

41. 576 U.S. (2015), 135 S. Ct. 2584(2015) (striking down same-sex marriage bans under the 14th Amendment to the U.S. Constitution).

42.   Letter from Attorney General Eric Holder to Speaker John Boehner (Feb. 23, 2011), at http://www.justice.gov/opa/pr/2011/February/11-ag-223.html.

43.   Rachel L. Swarns, *The Working Life: Placed on Unpaid Leave, A Pregnant Employee Finds Hope in a New Law*, N.Y. TIMES, Feb. 2, 2014, at http://www.nytimes.com/2014/02/03/nyregion/suspended-for-being-pregnant-an-employee-finds-hope-in-a-new-law.html.

44.   General Electric v. Gilbert, 429 U.S. 125 (1979).

45.   Pregnancy Discrimination Act, Pub. L. No. 95-555, 92 Stat. 2076 (1978) (codified at 42 U.S.C. § 2000e(k)).

46.   On comparisons in civil rights law generally, see Suzanne B. Goldberg, *Discrimination by Comparison*, 120 YALE L.J. 728 (2011).

47.   *See, e.g.*, Troupe v. May Department Stores Co., 20 F.3d 734 (7th Cir. 1994) (rejecting pregnant worker's claim because she didn't raise comparative evidence). The *Troupe* case is notable because the court invented a hypothetical comparator—a Mr. Troupe, who was likewise frequently tardy but not because of pregnancy—as a means of knocking down the plaintiff's claim. *Troupe*, 20 F.3d at 738.

48.   N.Y. HUMAN RIGHTS LAW § 296 (3)(a) (McKinney 2016) ("It shall be an unlawful discriminatory practice for an employer . . . to refuse to provide reasonable accommodations to known disabilities, or pregnancy-related conditions, of an employee, prospective employee or member in connection with a job or occupation sought or held or participation in a training program.").

49.   Rachel L. Swarns, *A Pregnant Worker, Forced to Go on Unpaid Leave, Is Back on the Job*, N.Y. TIMES, Feb. 26, 2014, at https://cityroom.blogs.nytimes.com/2014/02/26/a-pregnant-worker-forced-to-go-on-unpaid-leave-is-back-on-the-job/.

50.   Kelley Holland, *When Religious Needs Test Company Policy*, N.Y. TIMES, Feb. 25, 2007, at http://www.nytimes.com/2007/02/25/business/yourmoney/25mgmt.html.

51.   *This American Life, supra* note 1.

CHAPTER 6

1.   *See The Decathlon*, INTERNATIONAL ASSOCIATION OF ATHLETICS FEDERATION, *at* https://www.iaaf.org/disciplines/combined-events/decathlon.

2.   Sean Gregory, *The World's Greatest Athlete Wins Gold in London. And So Does Usain Bolt. Is Decathlete Ashton Eaton Really Better than Bolt?*

Time, Aug. 9, 2012, *at* http://olympics.time.com/2012/08/09/the-worlds-greatest-athlete-wins-gold-in-london-and-so-does-usain-bolt-is-decathlete-ashton-eaton-really-better-than-bolt/.

3. *Id.*
4. The following comes from Arash Markazi, *How Bruce Jenner Became an Olympic Icon Exactly 39 Years Ago*, ESPN, July 30, 2015, *at* http://www.espn.com/olympics/story/_/id/13346959/bruce-jenner-became-olympic-icon-exactly-39-years-ago; A.J. Baime, *The Fast Times of Caitlyn Jenner, Race Car Driver*, The Drive, May 19, 2016, *at* http://www.thedrive.com/accelerator/3557/the-fast-times-of-caitlyn-jenner-race-car-driver; Barry McDermott, *Back to Bruce in a Moment. First This Commercial*, Sports Illustrated, Sept. 26, 1977, *available at* https://www.si.com/vault/1977/09/26/622725/bruce-jenner-advertising-1976-olympics#; Mike Vaccaro, *Remembering the Bona Fide Superstar Bruce Jenner Once Was*, New York Post, June 1, 2015, *at* http://nypost.com/2015/06/01/remembering-the-bona-fide-superstar-bruce-jenner-once-was/.
5. *Bruce Jenner: The Interview*, ABC News, *at* http://abcnews.go.com/2020/fullpage/bruce-jenner-the-interview-30471558.
6. Buzz Bissinger, *Caitlyn Jenner: The Full Story*, Vanity Fair, July 2015, *at* http://www.vanityfair.com/hollywood/2015/06/caitlyn-jenner-bruce-cover-annie-leibovitz.
7. Tessa Stuart, *Meet the Trans Woman Challenging Caitlyn Jenner on Her Conservatism*, Rolling Stone, March 8, 2016, *at* http://www.rollingstone.com/politics/news/meet-the-trans-woman-challenging-caitlyn-jenner-on-her-conservatism-20160308.
8. Richard Pérez-Peña, N.Y. Times, June 12, 2015, *at* https://www.nytimes.com/2015/06/13/us/rachel-dolezal-naacp-president-accused-of-lying-about-her-race.html.
9. Mitchell Sunderland, *In Rachel Dolezal's Skin*, Broadly, Dec. 7, 2015, *at* https://broadly.vice.com/en_us/article/rachel-dolezal-profile-interview.
10. http://www.mirror.co.uk/news/world-news/rachel-dolezal-disgraced-race-activist-5901170.
11. Caitlin Keating, *Rachel Dolezal Says She Was 'a Little Too Black' for her African-American Ex-Husband*, People, March 27, 2017, *at* http://people.com/books/rachel-dolezal-ex-husband-black-new-memoir/.
12. *Rachel Dolezal Breaks Her Silence: 'I Identify as Black,'* Today, June 16, 2015, *at* http://www.today.com/video/rachel-dolezal-breaks-her-silence-i-identify-as-black-465269315945.

13. Elizabeth Harris, *Barnard College, After Much Discussion, Decides to Accept Transgender Women*, N.Y. TIMES, June 4, 2015, *at* https://www.nytimes.com/2015/06/05/nyregion/barnard-college-to-accept-transgender-women.html.

14. *Transgender Admissions Policy & FAQ*, BARNARD COLLEGE, at https://barnard.edu/admissions/transgender-policy.

15. *Id.*

16. *Id.*

17. Meredith Bennett-Smith, *Smith College Rejects Female Transgender Student Calliope Wong; Applicant Ruled 'Male' By Admissions*, HUFFINGTON POST, Mar. 21, 2013, *at* http://www.huffingtonpost.com/2013/03/21/smith-college-transgender-calliope-wong_n_2920845.html.

18. *Id.*

19. *Gender Identity & Expression*, SMITH COLLEGE, *at* https://www.smith.edu/about-smith/diversity/gender-identity-expression.

20. *Mission and Gender Policy*, WELLESLEY COLLEGE, *at* http://www.wellesley.edu/news/gender-policy#DTKDOE4uvWWVQQs2.97.

21. *Admission of Transgender Students*, MOUNT HOLYOKE, *at* https://www.mtholyoke.edu/policies/admission-transgender-students.

22. *Policy on Transgender Issues*, HOLLINS UNIVERSITY, *at* https://www.hollins.edu/on-campus/student-life/new-student-info/policy-on-transgender-issues/.

23. *Mission Statement*, BARNARD COLLEGE, *at* https://barnard.edu/about/vision-values.

24. Decca Aitkenhead, *Rachel Dolezal: 'I'm not going to stoop and apologise and grovel*, THE GUARDIAN, Feb. 25, 2017, *at* https://www.theguardian.com/us-news/2017/feb/25/rachel-dolezal-not-going-stoop-apologise-grovel.

25. Charles M. Blow, *The Delusions of Rachel Dolezal*, N.Y. TIMES, June 17, 2015, *at* https://www.nytimes.com/2015/06/18/opinion/charles-blow-the-delusions-of-dolezal.html.

26. *Id.*

27. After struggling to find the case in traditional legal databases, I found the opinion here: *NAACP Imposter Sued School over Race Claims*, THE SMOKING GUN, June 15, 2015, *at* http://thesmokinggun.com/file/rachel-dolezal-lawsuit.

28. Aitkenhead, *Not Going to Stoop, supra* note 24.

29. Law professor Camille Gear Rich makes this argument in a rare defense of Rachel Dolezal. Camille Gear Rich, *Rachel Dolezal Has a Right*

to *Be Black*, CNN, June 15, 2015, *at* http://www.cnn.com/2015/06/15/opinions/rich-rachel-dolezal/.

30. *See, e.g.*, Loving v. Virginia, 897 U.S. 113 (1973) (using strict scrutiny to strike down Virginia's anti-miscegenation statute under the 14th Amendment).

31. *See, e.g.*, Grutter v. Bollinger, 539 U.S. 306, 326–327 (2003) (laying out the strict scrutiny standard in a case involving race-based admissions at the University of Michigan's law school); United States v. Virginia, 518 U.S. 515, 531–534 (1996) (laying out the intermediate scrutiny standard in a case involving sex segregation at the Virginia Military Institute).

32. United States v. Carolene Products Co., 304 U.S. 144, 152 n.4 (1938).

33. *Id.*

34. San Antonio Independent School District v. Rodriguez, 411 U.S. 1, 28 (1973) (wealth discrimination); Massachusetts Board of Retirement v. Murgia, 427 U.S. 307, 313 (1976) (age); Cleburne v. Cleburne Living Center, Inc., 473 U.S. 432, 442 (1985) (mental disabilities); Lyng v. Castillo, 477 U.S. 635, 638 (1986) (food stamps).

35. On both of these points, see J. Harvie Wilkinson, *The Supreme Court, the Equal Protection Clause and the Three Faces of Constitutional Equality*, 61 VA. L. REV. 945 (1975).

36. Samuel R. Gross et al., *Race and Wrongful Convictions in the United States*, THE NAT. REGISTRY OF EXONERATIONS, March 7, 2017, at https://www.law.umich.edu/special/exoneration/Documents/Race_and_Wrongful_Convictions.pdf. For coverage of the study, see Niraj Chokshi, *Black People More Likely to Be Wrongfully Convicted of Murder, Study Shows*, N.Y. TIMES, March 7, 2017, *at* https://www.nytimes.com/2017/03/07/us/wrongful-convictions-race-exoneration.html.

37. I say "principal" as a means of distinguishing specific parts of the doctrine, the exceptions to the basic rule. Here I'm thinking about voluntary affirmative action programs, which are possible under the statute despite seeming like violations of the text. *See, e.g.*, United Steelworkers of America v. Weber, 443 U.S. 193 (1979); Johnson v. Transportation Agency, Santa Clara County, California, 480 U.S. 616 (1987).

38. I am intentionally alluding to the anticlassification/antisubordination debate in equality law. *See generally* Owen M. Fiss, *Groups and the Equal Protection Clause*, 5 PHIL. & PUB. AFF. 107 (1976) (distinguishing between two ways of doing equality).

39. *See, e.g.*, St. Mary's Honor Center v. Hicks, 509 U.S. 502, 527 (1993) (describing "protected class" as part of the prima facie case for intentional discrimination).

40. 42 U.S.C. § 2000e-2(a)(1) ("It shall be an unlawful employment practice for an employer to fail or refuse to hire or to discharge any *individual*, or otherwise to discriminate against any *individual* with respect to his compensation, terms, conditions, or privileges of employment, because of such *individual*'s race, color, religion, sex, or national origin") (emphasis added).

41. IT GETS BETTER PROJECT, *at* http://www.itgetsbetter.org/.

42. Full disclosure: The language in this paragraph is based on one of my earlier writings. *See* Zachary A. Kramer, *The New Sex Discrimination*, 63 DUKE L.J. 891, 945–946 (2014).

43. Mitch Kellaway, *REPORT: Trans Americans Four Times More Likely to Live in Poverty*, THE ADVOCATE, Feb. 18 2015, *at* http://www.advocate.com/politics/transgender/2015/02/18/report-trans-americans-four-times-more-likely-live-poverty. The story discusses a report by the Movement Advancement Project and Center for American Progress, *Paying an Unfair Price: The Financial Penalty for Being Transgender in America*, *at* http://www.lgbtmap.org/unfair-price-transgender.

44. Luke Malone, *Transgender Suicide Attempt Rates Are Staggering*, VOCATIV, March 5, 2015, *at* http://www.vocativ.com/culture/lgbt/transgender-suicide/.

45. *A Matter of Life and Death: Fatal Violence Against Transgender People in America 2016*, HUMAN RIGHTS CAMPAIGN & TRANS PEOPLE OF COLOR COALITION, *at* http://hrc-assets.s3-website-us-east-1.amazonaws.com//files/assets/resources/A-Matter-of-Life-and-Death-2016.pdf.

46. Bissinger, *Caitlyn Jenner: The Full Story, supra* note 6.

47. Julie Miller, *Rhianna Praises Rachel Dolezal: "I think She Was a Bit of a Hero,"* VANITY FAIR, Oct. 6, 2015, *at* http://www.vanityfair.com/hollywood/2015/10/rihanna-rachel-dolezal.

48. *Id.*

49. Christian Datoc, *MSNBC Guest: More Black People Support Rachel Dolezal Than Clarence Thomas*, THE DAILY CALLER, June 16, 2015, *at* http://dailycaller.com/2015/06/16/msnbc-guest-more-black-people-support-rachel-dolezal-than-clarence-thomas-video/.

50. *Id.*

51. Rich, *Rachel Dolezal Has a Right to Be Black, supra* note 29.

52. *Id.*

53. *Id.*

54. Ta-Nehisi Coates, *An American Kidnapping*, THE ATLANTIC, June 17, 2015, *at* https://www.theatlantic.com/politics/archive/2015/06/kalief-browder/395963/.

55. Jennifer Gonnerman's *New Yorker* piece about Kalief Browder should be required reading for everyone interested in race and criminal justice and the state of punishment in America. *See* Jennifer Gonnerman, *Before the Law*, THE NEW YORKER, Oct. 6, 2014, at http://www.newyorker.com/magazine/2014/10/06/before-the-law.

56. Coates, *Kidnapping, supra* note 54.

57. CLAUDIA RANKINE, CITIZEN: AN AMERICAN LYRIC 68 (2014)

58. David Ulin, *The Art of Poetry No. 102: Claudia Rankine*, THE PARIS REV. 219 (Winter 2016) (interview), *available at* https://www.theparisreview.org/interviews/6905/claudia-rankine-the-art-of-poetry-no-102-claudia-rankine.

59. *Id.*

60. RANKINE, CITIZEN, *supra* note 57, at 14.

61. *Id.*

62. RANDALL KENNEDY, NIGGER: THE STRANGE CAREER OF A TROUBLESOME WORD (2002).

63. Chris McGreal, *Rachel Dolezal: 'I wasn't identifying as black to upset people. I was being me,'* THE GUARDIAN, Dec. 13, 2015, *at* https://www.theguardian.com/us-news/2015/dec/13/rachel-dolezal-i-wasnt-identifying-as-black-to-upset-people-i-was-being-me.

CHAPTER 7

1. The print was designed by artist Dan O. Williams for *N+1*, a literary journal based in New York. The print can be seen here: https://fontsinuse.com/uses/14425/utopia-in-our-time-poster

2. Peter Haldeman, *My Father, the Shapeshifter*, N.Y. TIMES, Dec. 31, 2016, at https://www.nytimes.com/2016/12/31/fashion/susan-faludi-father-in-the-darkroom.html?_r=0. The following is drawn from Haldeman's article, as well as from Jennifer Senior, *Father Was a Vicious Bully. Then He Became a Woman*, N.Y. TIMES, June 12, 2016 (Reviewing SUSAN FALUDI, IN THE DARKROOM (2016)), at https://www.nytimes.com/2016/06/13/books/review-susan-faludi-in-the-darkroom.html.

3. Susan Faludi, *The Reckoning: Safeway LBO Yields Vast Profits but Exacts a Heavy Human Toil*, WALL ST. J. May 16, 1990.

4. SUSAN FALUDI, THE TERROR DREAM: MYTH AND MISOGYNY IN AN INSECURE AMERICA (2007).

5. SUSAN FALUDI, BACKLASH: THE UNDECLARED WAR AGAINST AMERICAN WOMEN (1991).

6. SUSAN FALUDI, STIFFED: THE BETRAYAL OF THE AMERICAN MAN (1999).
7. Haldeman, *My Father, the Shapeshifter, supra* note 2.
8. SUSAN FALUDI, IN THE DARKROOM (2016).
9. Pronouns matter, of course, and I don't want to offend or confuse. I'm taking my cue from Stefánie Faludi herself, who never stopped referring to herself as Susan's father. "A normal family stays together. I'm still your father," Stefánie said to Susan during their initial phone call. FALUDI, IN THE DARKROOM, *supra* note 8, at 20. For her part, Susan Faludi alternates between "she" and "my father" throughout the book. As she told a reporter, it was a copyeditor's nightmare. Haldeman, *My Father, the Shapeshifter, supra* note 2.
10. FALUDI, IN THE DARKROOM, *supra* note 8, at 416.
11. *Id.*
12. This test grows out of the Supreme Court's conscientious objector jurisprudence. *See* United States v. Seeger, 380 U.S. 163 (1965); 398 U.S. 333 (1970). The EEOC has likewise concluded that religion under Title VII includes "moral and ethical beliefs as to what is right and wrong which are sincerely held with the strength of traditional religious views." 29 C.F.R. § 1605.1 (2013).
13. Peterson v. Wilmur Communications, Inc., 205 F. Supp. 2d 1014 (E.D. Wisc. 2002).
14. *Id.*
15. *Id.*
16. *See, e.g.*, E.E.O.C. v. Unión Independiente de la Autoriadad de Acueductos y Alcantarillados de P.R., 279 F.3d 49, 56 (1st Cir. 2002); E.E.O.C. v. Ilona of Hungary, Inc., 108 F.3d 1569, 1575 (7th Cir. 1997); Redmond v. GAF Corp., 574 F.2d 897, 901n.12 (7th Cir. 1978).
17. Hussein v. The Waldorff-Astoria, 134 F. Supp. 2d 591 (S.D.N.Y. 2001)
18. *Id.* at 596–598.
19. Legal philosopher Brian Leiter doesn't think so. *See* BRIAN LEITER, WHY TOLERATE RELIGION (2012). Professor Micah raises a similar question. *See* Micah J. Schwartzman, *What if Religion Is Not Special?* 79 U. CHI. L. REV. 1351 (2012).
20. CHERYL STRAYED, WILD: FROM LOST TO FOUND ON THE PACIFIC CREST TRAIL 157 (2012).
21. Marks v. Nat'l Comm. Assoc., Inc., 72 F. Supp. 2d 322, 326 (S.D.N.Y. 1999). My introduction to Deborah Marks came from Professor Anna Kirkland's excellent discussion of the case. *See* ANNA KIRKLAND, FAT RIGHTS: DILEMMAS OF DIFFERENCE AND PERSONHOOD (2008).

22. *Marks*, 72 F. Supp. 2d at 326.

23. The following borrows from three sources. *See* Eli Saslow, *The White Flight of Derek Black*, Wash. Post, Oct. 15, 2016, *at* https://www. washingtonpost.com/national/the-white-flight-of-derek-black/2016/ 10/15/ed5f906a-8f3b-11e6-a6a3-d50061aa9fae_story.html?utm_ term=.689df6603df6; Elon Green, *Behind the Story: 'The White Flight of Derek Black,'* Colum. Journalism Rev., Dec. 13, 2016, *at* https:// www.cjr.org/the_feature/eli_saslow_derek_black_longform.php; R. Derek Black, *Why I Left White Nationalism*, N.Y. Times, Nov. 26, 2016 (Opinion), *at* https://www.nytimes.com/2016/11/26/opinion/sunday/ why-i-left-white-nationalism.html?_r=0.

24. I must confess some discomfort with the term white nationalism. That has come to have special meaning within our current political environment, which muddies the waters considerably. I could have easily used the phrase white supremacy or just called it a website that peddles in hate.

25. Email from Derek Black to Mark Potok, Senior Fellow, Southern Poverty Law Center (July 15, 2013), *at* https://www.splcenter.org/sites/ default/files/derek-black-letter-to-mark-potok-hatewtach.pdf.

26. *Id.*

27. *Id.*

28. 42 U.S.C. § 2000e(j).

29. Trans World Airlines, Inc. v. Hardison, 432 U.S. 63, 67 (1977).

30. Marks v. Nat'l Comm. Assoc., Inc., 72 F. Supp. 2d 322, 326 (S.D.N.Y. 1999).

31. This is, of course, a riff off of Justice Brennan's famous line, in dissent, in *McCleskey v. Kemp*. There, the Court rejected evidence of racial bias in the administration of the death penalty, to which Brennan said the majority's reasoning betrayed "a fear of too much justice." McCleskey v. Kemp, 481 U.S. 279, 339 (Brennan, J., dissenting).

32. Adam Liptak, *Muslim Woman Denied Job Over Head Scarf Wins in Supreme Court*, N.Y. Times, June 2, 2015, at A8.

33. *Id.* (noting that, at trial, Elauf called the mall "second home").

34. E.E.O.C. v. Abercrombie & Fitch Stores, Inc., 575 U.S. __ (2015), 135 S. Ct. 2028 (2015).

35. *Id.* at 2032–2033.

36. *Id.* at 2033–2034.

37. Cynthia Estlund, Working Together: How Workplace Bonds Strengthen A Diverse Democracy (2003).

CONCLUSION
1. Dale Hansen, *Hansen Unplugged: Celebrating Our Differences*, Feb. 12, 2014, at https://www.youtube.com/watch?v=Pjc6QlIdGg4.
2. In other installments, Hansen addressed violence between police and people of color (http://www.wfaa.com/sports/dale-hansen/hansen-unplugged-an-attack-on-our-basic-humanity/268208869), a transgender high school wrestler (http://www.wfaa.com/news/hansen-unplugged-transgender-euless-trinity-wrestler/415793677), and sexual violence and college sports (http://www.wfaa.com/sports/dale-hansen/unplugged-on-mulkeys-controversial-comments-she-sounds-tone-deaf/415289311), among others.
3. John Branch, *N.F.L. Prospect Michael Sam Proudly Says What Teammates Knew: He's Gay*, N.Y. TIMES, Feb. 9, 2014, at A1.
4. The St. Louis Rams eventually drafted Sam, as the 249th overall pick in the draft. Nick Wagoner, *Michael Sam: 'Overwhelmed' by pick*, ESPN, May 12, 2014, at http://www.espn.com/nfl/draft2014/story/_/id/10913755/2014-nfl-draft-michael-sam-drafted-st-louis-rams-seventh-round.
5. I struggled mightily to source this quote. A number of websites cite Lorde's 1994 book *Our Dead Behind Us*, but I didn't find it there. My attempt to crowdsource the quote turned up nothing. Then I sought the help of two librarians, both of whom struck out. The closest I came—with the help of ASU librarian Tara Mospan—was this statement from Lorde: "Certainly there are very real differences between us of race, age, and sex. But it is not those differences between us that are separating us. It is rather our refusal to recognize those differences, and to examine the distortions which result from our misnaming them and their effects upon human behavior and expectation." Audre Lorde, *Age, Race, Class, and Sex: Women Redefining Difference*, in SISTER OUTSIDER: ESSAYS AND SPEECHES 114, 115 (1984).

INDEX